MW00523218

CHRISTIAN GROWTH SERIES
LEADER'S GUIDE

COMMITMENT TO GROWTH

CONGRATULATIONS! YOU ARE GIFTED!

GETTING IT TOGETHER

BUILDING RELATIONSHIPS WITH GOD & OTHERS

Jim Burns
Doug Webster
Doug Fields
David Olshine

HARVEST HOUSE PUBLISHERS
Eugene, Oregon 97402

Other books by Jim Burns:

Building Relationships...with God and Others
Congratulations! You Are Gifted!
Getting It Together
Giving Yourself to God
Commitment to Growth
Living Your Life...As God Intended
Putting God First
Making Your Life Count
Handling Your Hormones, "The Straight Scoop on Love and Sexuality"
High School Ministry (co-authored with Mike Yaconelli)

Unless otherwise stated, Scripture quotations are from the New American Standard Bible.

LEADER'S GUIDE II

Copyright © 1986 by Harvest House Publishers
Eugene, Oregon 97402

ISBN 0-89081-555-0

All rights reserved. No portion of this book may be reproduced in any form without the written permission of the Publisher.

Printed in the United States of America.

With special thanks to
Doug Fields
David Olshine
and Doug Webster
for their contribution to this Leader's Guide

CONTENTS

CHRISTIAN GROWTH SERIES LEADER'S GUIDE

Introduction

Each week millions of teenagers will meet in Christian youth groups around the country. The groups will vary in size and shape, and even in doctrine. It is a fact that most kids desire to learn more about God and how He relates to their world. It is also true that many of those kids will walk out of their youth groups *bored!* Sometimes they are bored because of their poor attitudes; other times they are bored because you and I, as leaders, did not help lead them toward effective learning.

As their leader you are the most important ingredient in a successful learning situation. You do not have to be dynamic, funny, good-looking, or even a Bible scholar, but you do need to have a genuine desire to love and care for young people. Building a loving, relational friendship with the young people in your group is probably more important than anything you teach them. In fact, the way you care for them will teach a lot about God's love and care for them as well.

Here are a few helpful reminders for you as a leader. People learn experientially. *We learn by doing!* This means we must keep our meetings practical and look for ways our students can discover the truth of God for themselves. Since we all learn and are motivated in different ways, use as much variety as possible in teaching methods. Create a warm and friendly environment to set the proper mood for learning. Then make sure there is lots of discussion and interaction. You might even throw in some tension in order to raise questions to help them digest what they've been learning. And whatever you do, don't get involved in doing the same old teaching style week after week.

Be creative and change your methods of teaching to adapt to the lesson. Sometimes bring a guest speaker, a specialist in the area you are studying.

Other times do a role play or a simulative game. Use of various types of media, whether it be through films, records or the newspaper, make wonderful discussion starters. Field trips are great learning strategies. Let your imagination run wild and you'll come up with very good learning experiences that will dare your students to not be bored.

This Leader's Guide is divided into five areas for each chapter to assist you at making each chapter come alive to your students. Here is some great advice: Don't follow this guide exactly! Use it as a resource for ideas. Some of the suggestions will fit your group perfectly and others won't. There is enough material to do a series of meetings for one chapter or you might want to skip a chapter entirely. I believe the best teaching would happen if each member had his or her own workbook to write in and work through.

Here's how the Leader's Guide works:

1. *The Big Idea*—This is simply the main thought or theme for the chapter. It will help you form your reason for teaching each particular lesson.

2. *Using the Workbook*—In this section I simply walk you through the workbook. Be sure to read this section and adapt it to your own style.

3. *Related Scripture*—Here I've compiled several other Scriptures relating to the subject that were not covered in the workbook. It would be very helpful to look up these Scriptures as you prepare your lesson.

4. *Special Experiences*—We've added one special experience (at times we got carried away and added two) that is a proven success in youth groups related to the subject matter. Try them—they will help bring home the truth you are trying to teach them.

5. *Discussion Starters*—One of the best methods of learning is through discussion and we've written a number of discussion starters to help you lead an interesting and informative discussion.

Section 1

Commitment to Growth

———————

Contents

1. Walking in the Spirit

THE BIG IDEA

The Holy Spirit is the power and source developing the fruit of the Spirit in your life. Walking in the Spirit is to pursue a life-style led by the Spirit as defined in Galatians 5:22,23.

USING THE WORKBOOK

1. Explain the role of the Holy Spirit in the Old Testament and in the New Testament. Highlight how the Holy Spirit enters the life of a Christian.

2. Read Galatians 5:16-23 and discuss the questions on pages 7 and 8.

3. Compare and contrast the works of the flesh and the works of the Spirit in a modern setting.

4. Ask your group to dialogue on the different fruit and have each person choose one fruit he or she wishes to develop more.

RELATED SCRIPTURE

Ephesians 5:18   Romans 7:4-25   Matthew 7:7-11
1 Corinthians 3:16

SPECIAL EXPERIENCES

1. Take a Fruit of the Spirit inventory. On a scale of 1-10 (10 being the highest) have each person rate themselves according to the fruit. Discuss practical steps that will help each person develop the fruit.

2. Have each person write a letter to God regarding the fruit, their own prayer, and steps for improvement. Give them an envelope and have them self-address it and return it to the leader. The leader can wait six weeks or so and then mail the letter to the person.

DISCUSSION STARTERS

1. What does it mean to "walk in the Spirit"?

2. Which is easier: to "walk by the flesh" or "walk by the Spirit"? Why?

3. What obstacles stand in your way of becoming more fruitful?

4. How would you feel if someone described you by saying you are "loving, joyful, peaceful, patient..." (i.e. the fruit of the Spirit)?

5. How would your becoming more "fruitful" affect the lives around you?

6. What aspects of Jesus' life highlight the various fruit of the Spirit?

2. The Fruit of Love

THE BIG IDEA

God's love for us is unconditional. He loves us no matter what we do, who we are, etc. Understanding and experiencing God's love is the first step in developing the fruit of love.

USING THE WORKBOOK

1. God's love is very different from most of the love we see in our world. Use page 9 to compare and contrast various types of love.

2. Emphasize the type of love—agape love—that God has for us. Point out the two simple but powerful descriptions of God's love found on page 10.

3. Receiving God's love is not the end of the experience. God's love is to be shared. Use the agape love measuring inventory found on pages 10-12.

4. Seek to encourage not discourage each person with the inventory. Go beyond the inventory with your group by listing practical steps for improving each rating.

RELATED SCRIPTURE

John 15:12-17   Hosea 1:1-3; 3:1   1 John 4:7-8

SPECIAL EXPERIENCES

1. Tension Getter—A friend of someone in the group is considering marriage. She is 17 years old and a senior in high school. The marriage would mean dropping out of school and changing her life-style drastically. What would you say if she asked for your advice?

2. Play various popular love songs. Summarize the main idea of each song and compare it to God's agape love.

DISCUSSION STARTERS

1. Define love.

2. What does it mean to be "in love"? (Many people use "in love" as a criterion for marriage. When have I arrived at being "in love"?)

3. What type of love is exhibited most often in your home?

4. Respond to these statements:

   a. Falling in love is one of life's greatest experiences.

   b. Falling in love is a misconception.

   c. Romantic love is a myth.

5. What steps can you make to choose love instead of waiting for love?

3. Applying Agape Love

THE BIG IDEA

God's love for us is the *source* and *reason* for quality love relationships in our lives.

USING THE WORKBOOK

"Applying Agape Love" is a continuation of the previous chapter. It is the how-to's of putting God's love into action.

1. Summarize the discovery and definition of God's love from the previous chapter.

2. The chapter establishes three main aspects of God's agape love.

    a. **God's Love Means Commitments.** Discuss the experience Joshua must have had taking over Moses' job. Have each person discuss his feelings as if he were in Joshua's spot.

    b. **God's Love Must Be Communicated.** To say "I love you" is easy for some people and difficult for others. Discuss in your group why this might be true. Discuss the Scripture and questions on page 14.

    c. **God's Love Develops Community.** Discuss the Scripture and questions on page 14.

RELATED SCRIPTURE

Hebrews 13:5,6   Acts 2:42-47   John 21:15-19
Philippians 2:1-4

SPECIAL EXPERIENCES

1. Tell the group you need them for a "community survey." Have a few teams take a survey of surrounding homes. Ask the neighbors these questions:

    a. What comes to mind when you think of the word "community"?

    b. What are the most important ingredients of good relationships?

2. Have each person write a love letter to someone who needs to hear them say, "I love you."

3. Play Stevie Wonder's song "I Just Called To Say I Love You," then discuss it.

DISCUSSION STARTERS

1. Why is it so hard to remain committed to friends and family?

2. What is one thing you value very much? What would it take to give it up?

3. How often are you told "I love you"?

4. Ask the group the same questions found in the community survey.

4.   The Fruit of Joy

THE BIG IDEA

Joy is a trademark of Christians. Joy is not just happiness. Joy is the quality that remains consistent no matter what the circumstances may be.

USING THE WORKBOOK

This chapter is ideal for breaking up because of its length. The content could be divided into two studies. Another idea is to use the first half for the group and the second half as individual material. Thirdly, it will work well to divide the content into large-group then small-group settings.

1. It is important to distinguish between joy and happiness. Joy is consistent and steady. Happiness is based on experience and feelings. Make sure your group understands the true definition of joy.

2. Sections I and II point out the meaning of joy as discovered in the life of Christ. Discuss the birth, death, and resurrection of Jesus and the presence of joy.

3. Read and discuss John 15:1-11. Use the questions found on pages 16 and 17 to stimulate a practical and encouraging understanding of joy.

4. "Focus + Praise + Obedience = Joy"—Use the formula and helpful sections on pages 17 and 18 for action steps. Each of the three sections can be used for separate small groups. After completion of these sections, have the members of each group tell their answers to the rest of the groups.

RELATED SCRIPTURE

Philippians 4:4,5   Romans 12:12   Nehemiah 8:10
Jeremiah 31:13   1 Peter 1:8

SPECIAL EXPERIENCES

1. Role play either of the first two sections of the workbook, "The Object of Joy" or "The Action of Joy."

2. End your group with a time of "focus" and "praise." Have one person name a certain "focus" (i.e. God, Jesus, Holy Spirit, love) and have the rest of the group respond with short one-sentence "praises." For example:

   Leader: "Lord, we focus on Your love."

   Group: "Lord, I praise You for Your never-ending love."
   "Lord, I praise You for expressing love."

   Let the group pray for a while, then have the leader add a new focus, and continue with praises.

DISCUSSION STARTERS

1. How is joy different from happiness?

2. Can you be joyful and sad at the same time?

3. What makes joy such a rare quality?

4. What hinders you from being more joyful?

5. Who is the most joyful person you know? Why?

5. The Fruit of Peace

THE BIG IDEA

Peace is the contentment we feel as we stand before God cleansed and forgiven.

USING THE WORKBOOK

Many people suffer from lives that are anything but peaceful. The Holy Spirit delivers a tremendous gift to us when we receive His peace. Peace is the strength of letting God be God in our lives. As Paul writes, it is a "peace that surpasses all understanding." Peace is sometimes beyond understanding, explanation, and teaching but it is readily available for the Christian to experience. Strive to use this chapter experientially and emotionally more than intellectually.

1. The painting story on page 19 can be a valuable tool for portraying peace and introducing the chapter. Consider using it in conjunction with one of the Special Experiences listed for the chapter.

2. Peace must come from God before we see it in our own life. Read and discuss Section I on pages 20 and 21. The formula on page 21 is meant to stress the importance of confession and forgiveness as prerequisites to peace. Give your group time to understand the value and importance of confession. Consider a confession prayer time following Section I.

3. Word and deeds are two ways to express peace. Don't be afraid to let your group struggle with the idea of being peacemakers in our world of hate. Push for practical applications of peacemaking.

RELATED SCRIPTURE

Psalm 122:6-9   John 14:27   Psalm 34:14
James 3:18   Psalm 119:165   Hebrews 13:20

SPECIAL EXPERIENCES

1. Give each person time to create a peaceful setting. Encourage them to draw, write poetry or a short story, or cut and paste a collage from magazines.

2. Have a peace activity for fun or social involvement.

   For Fun: A car rally centering around the word "peace" (and "piece" as a play on words).

   For Social Involvement: Contact a local peace officer and have him or her speak to your group. Attend a local peace group meeting (i.e. Greenpeace, Neighborhood Watch, Volunteer Police/Sheriffs, Chemical Abuse Program). Possibly create a new peace group like the Student Peace Corps.

3. Watch a movie about Gandhi, Martin Luther King, or other non-violent leaders. Discuss their use of "peace" as a means of change.

DISCUSSION STARTERS

1. Where can you find peace in your world?

2. What do people mean when they say "I want peace and quiet"?

3. What keeps you from experiencing God's peace?

4. God forgives but oftentimes we cannot forgive ourselves. Why?

5. To what degree did Jesus mean "Blessed are the peacemakers"? Break up fights? Never argue? Not go to war?

6. The Fruit of Patience

THE BIG IDEA

Patience is not just putting up with someone or waiting your turn. Patience is the ability to see beyond people's weaknesses to help them discover who they can become.

USING THE WORKBOOK

1. Compare and contrast God's view of patience with the world's view of patience (pages 23-25). Help each person develop the mindset that God is eternally patient.

2. Discuss the following three practical steps for developing patience in your life:

   a. **View others as God views them.** Read the story of Zacchaeus. Describe Zacchaeus' character and the dislike people had for tax collectors. Emphasize the love and patience Jesus expressed to Zacchaeus. It is valuable to have each person think of Zacchaeuses in their lives. Ask them what it would take to see them as "Jesus in disguise."

   b. **Learn to cope with criticism.** Discuss various responses to criticism and then implement the helpful three steps found on page 26. Consider putting the steps on an index card and keeping it in your possession. Suffering from criticism shows a need to return to the Scriptures for a new mindset of God's patience.

   c. **Use your trials for growth.** Christianity does not remove trials—it teaches us to take advantage of them. This third point is a sign of growing maturity in a believer.

3. End the chapter with an evaluation of life by using the Patience Meter on page 27.

RELATED SCRIPTURE

Matthew 18:23-35   1 Timothy 6:11   Revelation 13:10
James 5:11

SPECIAL EXPERIENCES

1. Write a song about Zacchaeus. Write one song or divide into small groups and have each group write a song to a familiar tune. For example:

   (Sing to the tune of "5 foot 2, Eyes of Blue")

   > Five foot two, was a Jew
   > and a tax collector too,
   > Zacchaeus was a tiny man.
   >
   > Jesus was passing by,
   > All the others stood too high,
   > Zacchaeus was a tiny man.

2. Write a letter to Zacchaeus both before and after he met Jesus.

DISCUSSION STARTERS

1. Why does the list on page 23 demand your patience?

2. On a scale of 1-10 (10 being highest) rate the amount of patience expressed in your family.

3. Is your family the most demanding on your patience? Why? If not, then who is?

4. What is the opposite of patience?

5. Why do we criticize more than we affirm people?

7. The Fruit of Kindness

THE BIG IDEA

The life of Christ is the ultimate example of kindness. Kindness is the example of Christ acted out in a believer's life.

USING THE WORKBOOK

1. The poem in the beginning of the chapter (page 28) is written in reference to James and John's discussion with Jesus (Mark 10:35-45). Verse 45 is referred to in Section I of the chapter, but it would help to read the passage in Mark's gospel as a preface to the poem and the workbook chapter.

2. Read the Scriptures in Section I, "The Ultimate Example of Kindness." Use Mark 10:45 as a reference point for the example of Christ. Point out the extreme depth of God's kindness expressed in the cross.

3. Kindness is servanthood. It is love in action. Discuss the role of the servant found in Section II of the workbook.

4. The quote on page 30 is a powerful summary of one man's vision of kindness. The quote can be a valuable catalyst of group interaction.

5. The last line in the chapter encourages each person to make a list. Lists are wonderful if they precede doing. Don't let the group stop at lists. Use the chapter as a foundational point for beginning a new "kindness ministry."

RELATED SCRIPTURE

1 Samuel 20:14,15 Colossians 3:12 Jonah 4:2
Psalm 117:2 Ephesians 2:7 2 Peter 1:7

SPECIAL EXPERIENCES

Kindness is an action. Why not create an experience for the group to act out their kindness? Plan ahead for a short ministry experience to follow the study of the chapter. Some ideas include visiting a local rest home or rescue mission, helping serve a meal at a halfway house, visiting a friend or church member in the hospital, or cleaning someone's house (or one room if time is limited). The important element is not the specific act, rather the expression of simple kindness.

DISCUSSION STARTERS

1. Respond to each statement:

    a. "One person cannot make much of a difference. Why bother?"

    b. "You're too young. Wait until you have the wisdom and resources before you waste your time."

    c. "God helps those who help themselves."

2. Why does kindness stand out in our world?

3. How is the prayer, "Lord, make me . . ." different from, "Lord, give me . . ."?

4. What keeps you from starting or joining a "kindness ministry"?

8. The Fruit of Goodness

THE BIG IDEA

Goodness is the characteristic of a person who speaks and lives for good even if it means battling against evil.

USING THE WORKBOOK

Goodness is the nature of someone who lives for God in the midst of an evil world. For Christians to experience goodness, we must see it in God, contrast it to the world, and make it a life-style. This chapter strives to accomplish these three elements of goodness.

1. The opening story is a vivid picture of the presence or absence of someone striving for a pure, uncluttered flow of goodness. Discuss the unchanging truth of God's goodness pouring into our lives. God is not defined by what we consider good; rather, good is defined by what we know of God. Sections I and II portray goodness.

2. The debris must be removed in order for goodness to flow. Section III, Step One, "Define the Debris," helps us see the debris that exists in our own lives. A problem exists because many of us deny the existence of debris or evil in our lives. A close and more honest group will bring debris to the surface of the discussion. Be prepared for either in-depth sharing or revealing of life-styles by group members. It is also common for the opposite to occur. Seek to establish a supportive atmosphere that will enhance honest interaction.

3. Step Two on page 34 begins the final important ingredient for goodness: "Live the goodness." Priorities are a mirror of our choices. This step encourages each person to make "goodness" choices into a life-style. Encouragement—not guilt—is the objective of the exercise in setting priorities. Step Three, "Let Your Actions Speak Louder Than Your Words" is the push to "go and do."

RELATED SCRIPTURE

Micah 6:8   James 2:14-17   Colossians 3:17
Romans 8:28

SPECIAL EXPERIENCES

1. Collect magazines and read through them, separating the advertisements and articles on goodness from those of an evil or destructive nature. Discuss the world's influence on Christians.

2. **Confession Experience.** Have each person write down on a piece of paper struggles or sins that have entered his life. Take the folded papers in a sack, read 1 John 1:9, pray as a group, and then burn the sack.

DISCUSSION STARTERS

1. What would it be like to have the job of "the keeper of the spring"?

2. How can Christians define what is good and what is evil?

3. What keeps us from talking about the debris in our lives?

4. Are any group members Catholic? Discuss the value of a confession booth experience.

5. How literal is James 5:16?

9. The Fruit of Faithfulness

THE BIG IDEA

God is with us. His faithfulness causes us to become faithful, loyal people.

USING THE WORKBOOK

1. A proper understanding of God's faithfulness is a crucial foundation to a relationship with Him. "God is with me" on page 37 sums up the presence of God in the life of a believer. Use Section I, "The Faithfulness of God," to instill this doctrinal truth.

2. Section II provides five very practical points for developing faithfulness as a fruit of the Holy Spirit.

   a. **Keeping Promises**—Practical, biblical, and everyday questions and evaluations for the group. Use the graph on page 38 to instigate comparison of various areas of life and their various promise-keeping levels.

   b. **Trustworthiness**—Many people complain of others not trusting them. This section asks one key question. "Do you lead a trustworthy life?" Consider making 1 Corinthians 4:2 a memory verse for the chapter.

   c. **Responsibility**—One of the strongest proofs of maturity is a person's willingness to take responsibility for themselves. As Christians we are commanded to also take responsibility for others. The parable of the talents in Matthew 25 is ideal for discussion of responsibility. Have the group evaluate and rank the talents they possess.

   d. **Honesty**—This section uses an experience of knowing others who are real as an example of honesty. Without a doubt, people are attracted to real people.

e. **Commitment**—This section turns commitment back to our relationship with God. These four areas of God's Word, prayer, fasting, and tithing are vital signs of commitment. Some of these concepts might be very new to group members, so be prepared for questions.

RELATED SCRIPTURE

Hebrews 13:5   Psalm 40:10   Matthew 28:18-20
Lamentations 3:23

SPECIAL EXPERIENCES

1. Role play or dramatize the parable in Matthew 25:14-30. Consider modernizing it for a more relevant application.

2. Show the film "Face Value," distributed by Mars Hill Films, Waco, Texas.

3. Develop a certain project (start a church fund, sponsor a needy child, etc.) as a means to raise the tithing consciousness of the group.

DISCUSSION STARTERS

1. How does it feel to be at the receiving end of unfaithfulness?

2. Why are so many married people unfaithful to their spouses?

3. What happens to a relationship when you break a promise?

4. Why do many people turn their trust to false substitutes (drugs, alcohol, sex)?

5. Why does the word "responsibility" have such a negative connotation?

6. Why are we so spiritually inconsistent?

10. The Fruit of Gentleness

THE BIG IDEA

Jesus Christ's gentleness is the opposite of prideful living. The presence of Christ and the Holy Spirit move a believer toward meek living.

USING THE WORKBOOK

1. Compare and contrast the view of Jesus and Moses with the world's view of being macho. Realize that most of our society opposes "gentleness." Build the case for gentleness with the four insights about Moses and Jesus (pages 42,43). Read the various Scriptures, then contrast them with modern statements. For example:

   Bible: Matthew 5:5, "Blessed are the meek, for they shall inherit the earth."

   World: "Nice guys finish last."

2. Section II, "Modern Weakness," is where the rubber meets the road. All three points strive to elevate God and others above self. Section II is strong enough to use as a separate study at a later date. It might help to discover what elements keep us from being more submissive, more teachable, more selfless. Once again, read the listed Scriptures and seek to have the group interact with the Bible's command of gentleness. Can this be done in our modern world?

3. Colossians 3:12 contains priceless words of command to a gentle and meek life-style. Include verse 13 as another reminder of God's gentle approach to us that provides a path for forgiveness.

RELATED SCRIPTURE

Galatians 6:1   Psalm 131   Psalm 25:9
Titus 3:2   1 Peter 3:4

SPECIAL EXPERIENCES

1. Play parts of the famous movie, "The Ten Commandments," featuring Charlton Heston as Moses. Discuss the character of Moses in light of Numbers 12:3.

2. Do a character summary of various popular figures in our society in comparison with Moses and Jesus. Ask of each person these questions:

   a. What are his/her strongest characteristics?

   b. On a scale of 1-10 (10 being the highest) how meek is he/she?

   c. What part of me is like each of these people?
      (People examples: Rambo, Mother Theresa, John Wayne, Rocky, the President, the First Lady, etc.)

DISCUSSION STARTERS

1. Why do many males consider "meekness" a criticism, not a compliment?

2. What are the costs of living a life-style of gentleness?

3. Finish the sentence, "Sometimes it's hard to be last because..."

34

4. Why did Jesus choose a life-style of gentleness?

5. What attracts people to a gentle person?

11. The Fruit of Self-Control

THE BIG IDEA

Self-control is a process of yielding our lives to the Holy Spirit so He can make us more Christlike.

USING THE WORKBOOK

1. Have the group define self-control. Use this working definition as a theme throughout the chapter. Define self-control normally and then add a spiritual dimension to the definition. For example, a definition could be "The ability to channel resources to reach the desired goal." Add to it a spiritual dimension: "The Holy Spirit's power to channel all I am in order to become more Christlike."

2. A good definition is a natural beginning to Section I, "The Goal of Self-Control" (pages 46-47). Dialogue on the three points in this section. Ask the group to respond to the Thomas a' Kempis statement on page 47. Tie it in with 1 Timothy 4:7,8.

3. Read 1 Corinthians 9:25-27 stressing the importance of an athletic type of competition to reach our desired goal of Christlikeness. The four areas of self-control—physical, mental, emotional, and spiritual—are very practical sections for improving self-control. A few personal evaluations are included for more in-depth discussion. These evaluations are useful for small-group settings.

   a. The section on physical self-control is designed to be a tool for evaluation and accountability. Be careful not to overemphasize the ratings because many people, especially youth, criticize their physical life to the point of harmful destruction.

   b. Pay attention to the "emotional heat gauge" on page 49. Some people hide their emotions deep inside, others flaunt them easily, while a third group might discover release in areas of life previously buried by certain emotions.

4. Section III is a simple but helpful acrostic for reminding us to give our lives to God and gain more control of ourselves.

RELATED SCRIPTURE

Romans 7   Romans 12:1,2   Philippians 4:7
Ephesians 4:26,27

SPECIAL EXPERIENCES

Have one member of the group stand up in front of the others. He or she has to tell his or her life story in three minutes. In the meantime, have one or two members of the group try to break the speaker's control. If the speaker smiles or laughs, he is out. The antagonizers are not allowed to touch the speaker. Rotate various antagonizers with the same speaker. The experience emphasizes a person's strength of control.

DISCUSSION STARTERS

Rate the following scenarios on a response scale of 1-10.

    1-3   Blue—Cool
    4-7   Yellow—Frustrated
    8-10   Red—Ticked off

__ 1.   Someone is late to pick you up.

__ 2.   Someone forgets to call you.

__ 3.   A family member forgets your birthday.

__ 4.   Your parents argue all the time.

___ 5.   Nuclear war might occur before you die.

___ 6.   40,000 children die of starvation every day.

___ 7.   Your boyfriend/girlfriend breaks up with you.

___ 8.   Your parents might divorce or have divorced.

12. The Fruit of the Spirit Questionnaire

THE BIG IDEA

The fruit of the Holy Spirit is evidence of Christ in a believer.

USING THE WORKBOOK

The questionnaire is a whole chapter dedicated to the evaluation of a believer's fruit of the Spirit. The tool is designed to create awareness of areas of growth and areas of weakness. It is not a guilt inflicter. The chapter is meant to draw each person back to the power of the Spirit with thanks and supplication.

1. Have each person rate his or her life according to the individual characteristics of Christ, known as the fruit of the Spirit.

2. Star the areas rated 7 and higher for growth.

3. Check the areas rated 6 and lower for need of the Spirit's power.

4. Consider dating the inventory and checking back periodically as a way to be encouraged and accountable.

RELATED SCRIPTURE

Galatians 6:2   Romans 15:1   James 2:8

SPECIAL EXPERIENCES

1. Compare and contrast the group members' highs and lows. Match the people with highs in fruit with others who are low in the same fruit. Develop a spiritual training program to encourage growth in the weak.

2. Develop prayer teams who will ask the Spirit to produce more fruit.

3. Send out the questionnaires to various target groups (singles, children, families, seniors, college age, etc.). Summarize the information and send back ideas for growth in the weaker areas. Plan a fruit of the Spirit day or week.

DISCUSSION STARTERS

1. What is your strongest fruit? Why?

2. What is your weakest fruit? Why?

3. What hinders more growth?

4. Who do you know that is a living example of a fruitful believer?

Section 2

Congratulations! You Are Gifted!

Contents

1. Spiritual Gifts: Are They for Everyone?

THE BIG IDEA

All of us are gifted! God has given each one of us specific gifts that help in the effectiveness of the body of Christ.

USING THE WORKBOOK

Many of your students may feel that they aren't gifted. The goal of this chapter should be to help them understand that they are special and unique individuals whom God has gifted.

Take some time to explain how the body of Christ and the universal church work. Make sure they realize how significant their gift is to effectiveness within the body of Christ. Spend some time talking about how the body needs all of its "limbs" to function (1 Corinthians 12:12-26).

Have each student say where he/she thinks he/she might be gifted and what he/she might do to find out his/her spiritual gift.

They also need to know that once they realize their spiritual gifts they have got to learn how to put them into use to be effective in the body of Christ.

Something significant to understand are the four steps at the end of the chapter. Spend some time with each one of these (Experiment, Examine Your Feelings, Evaluate Your Effectiveness, Expect Confirmation from the Body of Christ), making sure that your students understand that even though they may want to have one of these individual gifts God may have a different one for them.

RELATED SCRIPTURE

Romans 12:6-8   Ephesians 4:7-12   1 Peter 4:9-11
1 Corinthians 12:28-30

SPECIAL EXPERIENCES

Break your group up into small groups (this can vary depending on the size of your group). Then give each group specific passages that will help them to list all the spiritual gifts that are found in the Bible. The gifts are found in these passages: Romans 12:6-8 (seven spiritual gifts); 1 Corinthians 12:4-11 (nine spiritual gifts); 1 Corinthians 12:28-30 (seven spiritual gifts); Ephesians 4:7,8,11,12 (five spiritual gifts); 1 Peter 4:9-11 (three spiritual gifts). Have the students list these gifts (you will find that some are repeated).

At this time you will want to explain (or have the students explain) how these spiritual gifts work for the benefit of the body of Christ (1 Corinthians 12:14-25). Explain how the different gifts complement each other for the strongest function of the body.

Give each group two different spiritual gifts (i.e. serving and knowledge) until all the gifts are distributed throughout the group. Each group must now define its spiritual gifts and how they function within the body of Christ. After they write this down they pass their spiritual gifts on to the next group and receive ones from another group.

The goal is for every group to define each gift (20 +) and its function within the body of Christ. It can be done in the form of competition to see which group finishes first. The challenge of competition can be exciting and can help make a positive point at the end of the game. The point is that no matter how fast a group may define and write out their answer they are dependent on the other groups to get their gifts, just as we are dependent on the spiritual gifts of others in the body of Christ.

DISCUSSION STARTERS

1. How do you know that you have been given specific gifts?

2. How can having knowledge about spiritual gifts positively affect a Christian?

3. Why do you think there are so many different types of spiritual gifts within the body?

4. How do you think that God chooses which gifts to give to each individual?

5. Where can the knowledge of spiritual gifts fit into your personal life? Youth group? Peer group?

2. Taking Time to Care

THE BIG IDEA

No matter what our gifts may be, we are all called into the ministry of serving and helping others.

USING THE WORKBOOK

Take time to brainstorm on specific areas in the church that couldn't take place if it weren't for the people who worked "behind the scenes" helping with preparation.

Ask the group why it is so difficult to play second fiddle. What are the feelings that make us want to be first fiddle and how do these attitudes run in contradiction to being a servant?

Jesus used the illustration of washing the disciples' feet to display servant-hood. Because of His culture (i.e. dirt and sandals) this was needed and relevant. Ask your group what they would do if they were to demonstrate, by example, servanthood.

Have each student share one area in which they struggle with being a servant (i.e. always eating first, wanting to sit in the front seat, etc.) and then assign another person to pray for that specific struggle and hold him/her accountable to that situation.

The story of the soldier, the hungry boy, and the donut is such a powerful story that it would be wise to spend some time talking about it. Ask the group if they *really* believe they can communicate God's love just because they give of themselves.

Have the group think of a media character that is portrayed as a servant. The idea behind this is that it is much easier to find the upfront person bringing attention to him/herself rather than the servant type. Ask the group why they believe this to be true of our media.

RELATED SCRIPTURE

James 4:10   Mark 9:33-37   Matthew 10:1-42
Matthew 23:10-12   Luke 22:26,27   Mark 10:35-45

SPECIAL EXPERIENCES

Here are some ideas taken from *Creative Bible Studies* published by Group Magazine:

1. Gather the class. Ask everyone to sit facing the center of the circle. Read John 13:2-20.

2. Use the towel to wipe the shoes of everyone in the circle. Do this from a kneeling position and in a caring and loving manner.

3. Ask the students to share feelings which must have gone through the minds of the disciples when Jesus washed their feet.

4. Pass the towels around the circle and have each person name an action that we, as disciples, do that soils the purity of Christ.

5. Pass out notebooks and pens. Ask the youth to reflect on this topic more deeply by noting occurrences in the past 24 hours of their lives that have been inconsistent with discipleship. Tell them that they will not have to show this material to anyone. Ask them to sit in different directions so that they are isolated from one another during this task.

6. Gather the group. Invite your people to share their general emotional responses to the task. What were the major feelings this consideration of Christ evoked?

7. Close by rereading the passage as the towel is passed around the circle. Give each person a strip torn from the towel.

DISCUSSION STARTERS

1. Is it a true statement to say that most Christians have a serving and helpful heart?

2. When you think of doing something helpful or positive without receiving praise what goes through your mind?

3. What is it that you enjoy about the people you would consider servants?

4. What are some specific things you can do to help your friends see that "looking out for number one" isn't always the best attitude?

5. After studying this section, what are some of the "thankless" jobs that you are going to start doing?

6. What is one activity or saying that will help remind you that we are called to be servants and helpers of the Lord?

3. Encouraging God's People

THE BIG IDEA

Exhortation is the unique ability to freely encourage as well as confront other people in order to lead them in the right direction.

USING THE WORKBOOK

Have each person in the group share the name of the person they chose as having the gift of encouragement. Then ask them how they feel when they are around this person.

Spend some time talking about the side of encouragement that we usually disregard: confrontation. How is it that encouragement and confrontation can go together?

Have your group spend some time brainstorming on the various situations that make it difficult to be people of encouragement.

Talk about why we need to be encouraged in what we do. Have your group think of specific instances in which they would have given up had they not received encouragement from someone else.

Ask the group what they thought of Barnabas. Oftentimes we focus on the "big names" of the Bible and Barnabas usually isn't mentioned. Who would they consider the Barnabas in the group?

RELATED SCRIPTURE

Isaiah 41:7	Acts 20:32	Matthew 25:34-40
Hebrews 3:12,13	1 Thess. 5:11-14	Romans 15:5

SPECIAL EXPERIENCES

Barnabas Award

Each week/month (depending on the size of your group) have the staff and the students vote on a Barnabas. Explain that this person is the one who is encouraging and helpful in the life of the youth group.

You may even want to go so far as making up Barnabas T-shirts or plaques that give further identification to the award winner.

Encouragement Circle

Have each student say something encouraging to every student in the group (you may want to break the group into smaller groups if it is large).

After this you may want to have the students share a "wish encouragement" with the group. A "wish encouragement" is something that shows concern and at the same time shows a desire for that person to be brought right. For example: "John, I wish that you might find the patience to deal with your parents because you have the tendency to become very angry when you are around them" or "Cindy, I wish you would discover the unconditional love God has for you so you would not work so hard at being loved."

As you can tell, this "wish encouragement" will be difficult to do in a group that has not spent much time together.

DISCUSSION STARTERS

1. Why is it difficult to be encouraging?

2. Who is one person that you can encourage this week at school, work, home, and church?

3. We have seen how Barnabas and Paul were encouragers. What are some ways in which Jesus encouraged those He was around?

4. Why is it difficult to confront someone even though you know it will help them get back on the right path?

5. The word exhortation means "to come alongside." After all that you have learned about encouragement, what do you think this will come to mean in your own life?

4. Giving It Away

THE BIG IDEA

A person with the gift of giving takes the focus off his/her personal "wealth" and places the focus on giving freely and cheerfully to the body of Christ.

USING THE WORKBOOK

Spend some time listing reasons why our society places such a great emphasis on money. Then list important qualities in life and see how many of these hold a monetary value.

Ask the students in your group where they spend the majority of their money. Most likely the majority of them will list things such as movies, video games, clothes, records, food, etc. Try to help them understand the balance Christians need in the distribution of their wealth.

The Attitude Checks are very straightforward and yet can appear ambiguous because they require such a drastic change in our life-style. Make sure you spend some time helping the students really understand what Scripture has to say about these specific areas of giving.

The story by the Unknown Confederate Soldier can make a person feel guilty. Talk about guilt and how some churches may use this form of motivation to get people to give. What Attitude Check does giving as a result of guilt fit under?

Have your group compare and contrast the gift of giving and the gift of serving (Chapter 3). Explore the ways in which they are similar, how they each affect the body of Christ differently, and the unique attitudes that these gifts need.

RELATED SCRIPTURE

2 Corinthians 9:11   1 Corinthians 16:2   Colossians 3:23,24
2 Kings 12:9

SPECIAL EXPERIENCES

Try one of these before the group starts:

Before your group meets have someone that none of the students will recognize dress up as a beggar and stand in front of the church asking for some type of handouts. Most of us would walk right by him/her. Have the students share feelings that they have when they are confronted by someone like this. You might even want to have your beggar friend come into the meeting and help lead some of the discussion.

Plan on giving some type of valued item to each student before the group starts (i.e. candy bar, movie ticket, etc.). If you are expecting ten students then only have nine of these valued items. Have one student that you previously talked to come in late to the meeting; he/she would be the tenth person. Watch how the group responds. Did someone offer to give or share his/her valued item? Or were they hanging on to theirs, pretending they did not know there were none left. Then talk about this in your discussion on giving.

DISCUSSION STARTERS

1. Why is it so difficult to give in secret?

2. How can money affect the way we view life?

3. What quality did the widow have that allowed her to give everything?

4. When you think of all that God has given you, how much do you think He will expect?

5. What type of giving attitude did God display when He gave Jesus to die for our sins?—see John 3:16. How does this relate to the type of giving presented in this chapter?

5. Building Up the Church

THE BIG IDEA

The church is built up through people who have the gifts of teaching and pastoring. These gifts help the body of Christ to grow spiritually.

USING THE WORKBOOK

Have the group brainstorm on specific qualities that make a teacher a great teacher. How should these qualities relate to teaching God's Word?

There is great responsibility in teaching from God's Word. Many people take it too lightly. James sets a precedent for teaching: "Let not many of you become teachers, my brethren, knowing that as such we shall incur a stricter judgment" (3:l). Have your group respond to this statement. Is this too severe?

Your kids will need to have experience with teaching if they are to ever know whether they have this gift or not. Try to figure out some times and places where they might be able to teach. They will need your supervision and guidance in their preparation.

The gift of pastoring will seem very distant and foreign to many of your students who feel that only older people who have had the proper schooling and training can have this gift. Let them talk about some of their preconceived understandings about this gift. How did they react when they learned this was a gift they might be able to have?

Spend some time explaining why Jesus uses the analogy of sheep and shepherd. Sheep aren't very smart animals (you've never seen one in a circus have you?) and need guidance. Shepherds help keep sheep together so that they don't go astray. How does a pastor do this same type of thing with his/her congregation?

Have the group come up with some specific ways in which they pastor some people or areas in the church. For example, maybe there are children with special needs with whom they can develop a relationship and spend time. Or they can help feed the hungry people on the street through serving a monthly meal. These ideas can build responsibility and give the students a sense of achievement where they feel that they are contributing to the sheep in the body of Christ.

RELATED SCRIPTURE

Micah 7:14   2 Samuel 5:2   Isaiah 40:11
John 10:2,11   Revelation 7:17   Hebrews 13:20

SPECIAL EXPERIENCES

For the Gift of Teaching

Have each one of the students prepare a message that they will teach to each other, to a group of people at a retreat, or at some other forum. Let them know that they are going to receive some type of input from one of the leaders that will be present. It might be wise not to let other students give formal evaluations of their teaching since it may be their first time. The evaluation should be affirming as well as constructive. You may even find that the other students will take in more from listening to their peers teach than they will when the leaders teach.

For the Gift of Pastoring

For those students who want to learn more about this gift, it would be wise to help them set up a time with the church's pastor and ask him/her questions about what it takes to be a pastor. You may need to help the students formulate some of the questions and be available to debrief them.

DISCUSSION STARTERS

1. How is it that the gift of teaching builds up the church more than other gifts? Or does it? (You may need to refer to chapter 1 to remind them that we are all gifted and that God uses all of us to build up the body.)

2. What are some of the requirements for being a teacher of God's Word?

3. Why is it that teachers are in such a vulnerable position when they are teaching?

4. Why is it that people need some type of pastor to help with their growth? Why can't they grow on their own?

5. What personality qualities do you think a pastor needs?

6. The Open Heart

THE BIG IDEA

The gifts of mercy and hospitality manifest themselves in individuals who are others-centered. These people focus on being sensitive to those who have needs.

USING THE WORKBOOK

Ask the group to give a present-day illustration of the Good Samaritan, using the school as the setting.

Have the group share personal illustrations of how they have used the gift of mercy in the past. Then talk about these examples. Are they the norm, or were they out of the ordinary? The person with the gift of mercy probably has those experiences regularly.

When talking about mercy, make sure you spend some time on the word compassion. Talk about situations that normally cause all of us to be compassionate.

Have the group list qualities that people who have the gift of hospitality possess. How are these qualities unique?

Make sure that the group knows the generosity involved in giving one's house up to meet the needs of others. It can be difficult at their age (since they aren't homeowners and don't care as much for privacy) to under-stand what is involved with being hospitable.

RELATED SCRIPTURE

Romans 12:13   1 Peter 4:9   Titus 1:8
1 Timothy 3:2   Hebrews 13:1-3

SPECIAL EXPERIENCES

Take your group to various organizations/institutions within the community that utilize the help of those with a compassionate heart. Volunteer some of your time to these organizations and then talk about how each one was different and what types of attitudes would be needed to work in these settings. A few examples of these might be rest homes, rehabilitation centers (drug, alcohol, physical, etc.), rescue missions, food lines, clinics (abortion, drug, child abuse, etc.), or various hospitals.

DISCUSSION STARTERS

1. What would our country be like if it was void of compassionate people?

2. Who is one specific person that you can show compassion to this week? What will you do?

3. Even if someone didn't have the gift of mercy as a spiritual gift, do you think it would be a necessary attitude for a Christian to strive after? Why or why not?

4. Why do you think it is difficult to be hospitable?

5. Are there a variety of ways in which the gift of hospitality can be used? If so, what are some of these ways?

7. Knowing Where to Go

THE BIG IDEA

The body of Christ needs certain men and women who have the gift of leadership and administration to help steer and direct others to action and goals.

USING THE WORKBOOK

One of the main themes of this chapter is to help the group understand that a leader isn't always the person up front. Take some time to brainstorm on various significant leaders in our world or in your youth group who aren't the stereotype of what we call leaders.

Spend some time talking about goals. Why are they important? What do they do to help stimulate the growth of a group? Take some time to set goals for your group and talk about how each person can take some form of leadership to help reach these goals.

Oftentimes there are selfish reasons for wanting to be a leader. Spend some time talking about Mark 10:35-41 and see if your group thinks this request of James and John was made from selfish motivation. List ways in which a leader can be accountable.

The football illustration is a great example of how administration and leadership differ. Have your group try to think of other illustrations that will help solidify the difference.

Discuss with your group the combinations of these gifts and how they work with one another and separately from one another. For example: "How is a leader without the gift of administration going to lead?" or "How is an administrator who doesn't have the gift of leadership going to be effective in the body of Christ?"

RELATED SCRIPTURE

Isaiah 48:17	Isaiah 63:14	Psalm 25:5
Psalm 61:2		

SPECIAL EXPERIENCES

Give your group a project (i.e. special event, retreat, or some other program) to organize, develop, and run. Give them some initial structure and meet with them regularly to see if they are surviving the awesome task.

Constantly be debriefing them on how the gifts of leadership and administration come into play during the planning. If you can give up some of the reins you will be very surprised at how much they will be able to do and how high quality the job will be. They will feel ownership in the program and group, and also gain a much greater respect for what you do as a leader.

DISCUSSION STARTERS

1. Why is it that we usually don't associate the term "leader" with "servant"?

2. After working through this chapter, how has your view of leadership changed?

3. In what ways was Jesus a leader to His disciples? To the crowds? To His enemies?

4. How can the gift of administration be helpful to a leader?

5. If someone didn't like to be in front of a group, could he/she still have the gift of leadership and administration?

8. Discovering the Right Path

THE BIG IDEA

The person with the gift of wisdom and/or knowledge has the unique ability to uncover insights that might normally be difficult to understand.

USING THE WORKBOOK

Ask your group to list some of the stereotypes that accompany wisdom (i.e. old, gray hair, slow talking). Then discuss how these stereotypes fall short.

The grocery list of wisdom found in Proverbs 2:1-12 is so thought-provoking that it is helpful to go through this one verse at a time and ask the group what each verse means.

Make sure that examples of both the gift of wisdom and the gift of knowledge are talked about and how each gift differently affects the body of Christ and your youth group.

People with these gifts can offer a positive degree of input to any given Bible study. Explore ways in which people with these gifts might have an unusual understanding of Scripture. Does this mean they will naturally have other gifts like teaching or pastoring?

RELATED SCRIPTURE

1 Kings 3:9   1 Kings 4:29   1 Kings 7:14
Proverbs 16:16   Ephesians 1:17   James 1:5

SPECIAL EXPERIENCES

Read a controversial story to your group and have them interact on it. This can be a good time to affirm their input and response to the story.

The following story is taken from the book *Tension Getters* published by Youth Specialties (page 45):

> Susan is not very attractive. People avoid her, and she can tell that most of the people she knows make fun of her behind her back. Quite frankly, she's ugly. She knows it and so does everyone else. She comes to you for help and advice.

DISCUSSION STARTERS

1. How can the gift of wisdom be helpful in dealing with people? With relationships? With the church?

2. If you have the gift of leadership, why is it important to surround yourself with people who have the gift of wisdom?

3. How is a person to search for wisdom? (Proverbs 2:4)

4. How can someone with the gift of knowledge be helpful to someone involved in a conflict?

5. What specific ways can you see God using the gift of knowledge in your youth group?

9. Sharing the Good News

THE BIG IDEA

The gifts of evangelism and prophecy communicate a truth—one is a truth *about* God and the other is a truth *from* God.

USING THE WORKBOOK

Many times young people associate evangelists with those who preach and ask for money on TV. They need to know that this is not the only type of evangelist that God uses to strengthen the body of Christ.

Have your group discuss the interesting dynamics that took place at the time of the Great Commission. Ask what their feelings might have been if Jesus was talking directly to them.

Someone with the gift of evangelism has a burden for the nonbeliever. Make sure your group realizes that the entire church needs to go to non-believers with a message about God.

The gift of prophecy is to help build up the church and the believer. This is very similar to the gift of exhortation. Discuss the similarities and differences with your group.

Ask the group what comes to mind when the word prophecy is mentioned. Do they receive negative or positive thoughts? Why is it that we often relate bizarre mystical thoughts with prophecy?

RELATED SCRIPTURE

1 Corinthians 14:3,5	Acts 2:17	Romans 12:6
Jude 14,15	Acts 19:6	Acts 8:40
Acts 23:11		

SPECIAL EXPERIENCES

Take the group to a hill and read Matthew 28:16-20. Then spend time listing specific ways they can reach their community for God. Have those with the gift of administration outline goals and directions for the group to take in order for them to experience the act of evangelism.

DISCUSSION STARTERS

1. Why is it often difficult to share the faith that is so special to you as an individual?

2. How would you feel if Jesus commanded you to take the Good News to your entire community? Could this possibly be the case with you now that you know what He told His disciples?

3. How does the verse "I am with you always, to the end of the age" (Matthew 18:20) help you during times of doubt over sharing your faith?

4. How does personal prophecy affect the body of Christ? Who receives the benefit—the body or the person?

5. How would the gift of prophecy fit into the life and function of your group?

10. Searching for a Sign

THE BIG IDEA

The gifts of tongues, healing, and miracles are more spectacular—not better—gifts that are used of God yet not very common to most of us.

USING THE WORKBOOK

The gifts of tongues and interpretation of tongues are very controversial gifts. We didn't want to present just one view, therefore eliminating others, but wanted to show what Scripture has to say about these gifts and let the students come up with their own belief system. You will want to use this chapter in a way that is helpful to your church's position on these gifts.

Find out where your group has heard of tongues or experienced tongues. See if they have a biblical understanding of what this gift is all about. So many times this special gift is misunderstood and abused because some groups unrealistically stereotype those who speak in tongues as more spiritual.

Have your group share some healing stories, both good and bad, that they have heard or experienced. Make sure they also share some of their feelings that accompany these stories. Do they believe them? Do they understand?

Through our present media there is usually a great emphasis on physical healing and little is ever said about the emotional healing that is very common. Make sure they understand the differences between the different types of healing.

So many of us ask God to perform miracles in our lives and when He does we often fail to notice and give Him recognition. We think of miracles as things such as raising people from the dead and walking on water. Ask your group what they think of individual miracles and flashy miracles.

RELATED SCRIPTURE

John 5:1-9   John 2:1-11   John 6:1-21
Acts 28:8   Luke 8:47   Mark 6:13
1 Peter 2:24   1 Corinthians 14:2   1 Corinthians 14:5
1 Corinthians 14:22 Acts 2:4   Acts 10:46

SPECIAL EXPERIENCES

Call the pastor of a charismatic church and see what takes place in their order of worship. If they are known to corporately share in tongues and experience miracles and healings, take your group to this church and let them visually experience these gifts firsthand. Make sure you spend time debriefing this experience to find out your group's response.

Ask a Christian doctor to speak to your group and share what he/she believes about healing, how he/she sees his/her role in the healing process, how it feels to watch someone die, and what part God's sovereignty plays in the healing process.

DISCUSSION STARTERS

1. How does the gift of tongues affect the individual believer? The body of Christ? Your youth group?

2. If speaking in tongues is a form of prayer, should this gift be used in your youth group?

3. How does healing benefit the body of Christ?

4. Is a Christian doctor the source of the healing in a patient, or is God? Explain why you answered the way you did.

5. What is one specific way in which you can help bring healing into someone's life this week?

6. What is one miracle that God has done in your life in the last year? Are you praying for God to work miracles in your life right now?

11.   Adventurous Faith

THE BIG IDEA

The gifts of faith and being an apostle requires a person to rely on God when the situation and/or journey seems difficult to believe in.

USING THE WORKBOOK

The gift of faith is a very ambiguous gift because it is difficult to measure in a concrete manner. You may need to help your group understand the difference between their personal faith and the gift of faith.

Have each person in the group list one of their favorite people from Hebrews 11 and why they liked this person.

After they have shared from Hebrews 11, have them tell you who they think is one person with the gift of faith (as they understand it) that they personally know. What aspects of that person's life illustrate the gift of faith?

Give your group some of the awesome statistics (available through world mission groups) that present the number of unevangelized people in the world who are overseas. This may help them understand that there is a need for people with this gift.

RELATED SCRIPTURE

Mark 5:34	Luke 5:20	Hebrews 11:6
Hebrews 13:7	Romans 10:17,18	1 Corinthians 15:9,10
Galatians 1:15-17	Colossians 1:24-29	1 Corinthians 1:1
1 Corinthians 12:27-31		

SPECIAL EXPERIENCES

Take your students on a faith walk where they have to walk a trail blind-folded holding onto the hand of another person who gives him/her directions. Afterward talk about the experience and how they had faith in the leader.

A faith fall is also another way to experience faith in someone. Have one person stand on something a few feet higher than the ground, fold his hands across his chest, and by keeping his back straight he is to fall freely into the group's hands that are waiting to catch him/her. If this person bends forward then he should do it again. Total faith is when the back is kept straight.

A fascinating experience is to interview a missionary (either retired or presently working). Ask about some of his/her experiences. How receptive were the nationals to the gospel? What were some of the traumatic experiences that occurred on the mission field? What luxuries were missed out on by going overseas?

Another idea is to take your group on a short-term mission and let them experience some of what it is like to be a missionary.

DISCUSSION STARTERS

1. Why is it difficult to have complete faith in God?

2. How would your life be different if you were to have the gift of faith?

3. What can one of your brothers or sisters in the Lord hold you accountable for when it comes to being more faithful?

4. When you think about going to a different country to spread God's message, what thoughts and feelings come into your mind?

5. If you were to go to another country because you were motivated by guilt, how do you think your ministry would be different from those with the actual gift of apostleship?

Section 3

Getting It Together

———————◆———————

Contents

1. Hey, I'm Different!

THE BIG IDEA

God is in the business of changing lives. God changed Paul. He can change you! This chapter shows us how to be different.

USING THE WORKBOOK

1. Take some time to look at Acts 7:54-60; 8:1 and Acts 9:1-9. Discuss the change that took place in Saul's (Paul's) life.

2. Dig into Romans 8:29. What is God's purpose for our lives? How does Jesus change us? Read Romans 12:1,2 and ask the youth, "In what areas has the world conformed you? How can you escape these pressures?"

3. Challenge the group to honestly deal with the question, "What three areas of your life would you like changed?" Ask the youth to share their answers. Then go over the pointers on being different (on pages 9-11).

4. The final section is extremely vital for reflection. Have the kids be open in their responses to the statements on page 11.

   a. I am open to let God change me. (yes, no, not sure)

   b. I will make the Bible my standard. (yes, no, not sure)

   c. I will surrender my life to the Holy Spirit. (yes, no, not sure)

Encourage your group to close in prayer, committing these above decisions to Christ's Lordship.

RELATED SCRIPTURE

Romans 8:29   Philippians 3:12-14   Romans 12:1,2
Proverbs 3:5,6

SPECIAL EXPERIENCES

The Great Button Controversy[1]

As an object lesson on conformity, put one or two dozen buttons in a box and pass it around the group. Have each student count the buttons and remember how many were in the box. By prior arrangement, the next-to-the-last person removes one button from the box secretly, so that the last person's count is off by one. When you ask the kids how many they counted, everyone will agree except for that one person (hopefully). In all probability, the different person will change his count to conform to the others, even though he is sure he is right. Follow up with a discussion on group pressure and denying your personal convictions in order to be accepted by the group.

DISCUSSION STARTERS

1. Why is it important to be different?

2. Why do you think it is so difficult to change?

3. How can you begin to actively change?

4. Take some time to list steps for change—short-term and long-term goals.

5. If there were one major area to change in your life, what would it be?

---

[1] *The Great Button Controversy* from *Ideas 9-12*, published by Youth Specialties, p. 76.

2. Getting Involved with God

THE BIG IDEA

Getting involved with another person takes time, listening, and sharing. In order to get involved with God, we must do the same.

USING THE WORKBOOK

1. Read Philippians 1:1-11. Dig into Philippians 1:4. Do you pray often?

2. Dive into the Prayer Test (page 14). Take some time to dialogue about the kids' prayer lives.

3. "If you were stuck in prison like Paul, would you be praying much? If so, for whom—yourself or others?" Talk about their responses.

4. Encourage the youth to make a specific goal from Philippians 1:3-11 (under the section "Application").

RELATED SCRIPTURE

Mark 11:24	Romans 12:12	Philippians 4:6,7
Matthew 21:22	Colossians 4:2	1 Thessalonians 5:17

SPECIAL EXPERIENCES

1. Try a prayer vigil. Enlist everyone to come to the church facilities or some designated place. Each person has a time slot of 15 minutes to a half-hour. The vigil can be several hours in total length.

2. Do a prayer candle. Turn the lights off. Pass a candle. As each person holds the candle he is encouraged to pray aloud. The others are praying quietly. The candle is passed in order for each person to participate.

DISCUSSION STARTERS

1. Do you like to pray? Why? Why not?

2. Why is it difficult to maintain a consistent prayer life?

3. Why do some enter into prayer easily and others have such a rough time?

4. Involvement means getting to know someone. What are some practical ways of getting closer to God through prayer?

5. Do you think you could make a commitment to pray five minutes daily? Explain. Will you go for it?

3.   Committed to What?

THE BIG IDEA

Every person is committed to something. In this chapter, we will discover some principles on Bible study, plus explore the question, "What are you committed to?"

USING THE WORKBOOK

1. Have the youth give a chapter title to Philippians 1. Then go around the room and share these titles.

2. Take some time going over *observation, interpretation,* and *application* questions. This type of inductive study is very critical for the young people to grasp. If they catch the style, they will be able to study the Bible on their own in the future.

3. Explain that application is the most important part of Bible study! Have them grapple with this section. Talk about the difficulty of applying Scripture to our lives.

4. Make sure the youth learn to ask themselves the question, "What does this passage say to *me*?" This helps internalize the passage.

RELATED SCRIPTURE

2 Timothy 3:15-17   2 Peter 1:19-21   Joshua 1:8
Psalm 119:1-19   Romans 10:17   Matthew 4:1-4

SPECIAL EXPERIENCES

For Better or for Verse[1]

Here is a possible way to form small groups for a retreat. Beforehand, choose some Bible verses and, depending on the number of people in the group, write a word or phrase from the verses on separate 3 x 5 cards. To identify the verses, place the "book" on one card and the "chapter and verse" on another. Finally, randomly distribute the cards and let the kids form the verses. Each group is created by the kids who hold cards from the same verse.

EXAMPLE: John 15:1

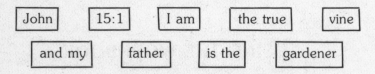

DISCUSSION STARTERS

1. How often do you read your Bible?

2. Do you have a difficult time reading the Bible? How about understanding it?

3. Which area is most easy: observation, interpretation, or application? Which is the most difficult?

4. What are some hindrances to effective Bible study?

5. What steps will you begin now to dive into God's Word?

---

[1] *For Better or for Verse* from *Ideas 13-16*, published by Youth Specialties, p. 93.

4. How's Your Conduct?

THE BIG IDEA

God calls us to endure suffering and live a life-style worthy of the gospel.

USING THE WORKBOOK

1. Have your kids discuss "What does it mean to suffer?" Let them share any times of suffering they have endured. Speak about Paul's view of suffering (Philippians 1:28-30).

2. Examine 1 Peter 1:5-7; 2:20,21; 4:12-14; 5:8-10. The writer, Peter, knows about suffering!

3. Look at the final section on pages 24-25 with the three "thoughts on having worthy conduct." This should be used to help the young people work on the issue of behavior and conduct. Placing these thoughts on an overhead projector or writing them on newsprint might be helpful. Have them repeat each principle:

   a. Don't be fearful of others.
   b. Salt your life-style.
   c. Light up someone's life.

4. Close by asking them to each seriously think about two non-Christian people who need some lighting up. Close in silent prayer for these two persons.

RELATED SCRIPTURE

Matthew 10:32,33   2 Timothy 1:7   Matthew 5:14-16
Colossians 4:5,6

SPECIAL EXPERIENCES

1. **Role Play.** Before the meeting, have two youths picked out for this drama. One is to play a Christian, the other a "nasty" non-Christian. The Christian attempts to witness of his faith to the nonbeliever. These two will role play in front of the group for about three minutes. The non-Christian is very offensive and "out-duels" the Christian in a debate about Christianity. Examples: "There are too many hypocrites . . . ," "The Bible is a fairytale . . . ," etc. A discussion should follow about the feelings of the Christian as he was "ripped to shreds" by the nonbeliever.

   Some questions: 1. How did the Christian withstand persecution?

   2. Could the Christian have been more "offensiv

   3. How is the Christian to respond to suffering this?

2. **Discipleship**[1] (Luke 14:25-35)

   Focus: The cost.

   Preparation: You will need a broom or mop handle for each student. Bring a piece of cloth about two feet square. You also will need several small scraps of paper and a pencil for each person.

   Insight: Jesus teaches His followers about the cost of discipleship. He tells them that they must be willing to separate themselves from their families and follow Him if it is demanded.

   They must be prepared to bear their own crosses just as Christ will do so. They would not undertake the construction of a tower if they did not have adequate resources. People would laugh at such a folly. Likewise, a king will not go to war without being sure he has the resources to be successful. If he doesn't, he will attempt to make peace.

   Therefore, a disciple must give up *all* possessions to be a follower of Jesus. This teaching challenges the concept of "cheap" or easy grace. Jesus is offering a tough faith.

   In this study, the youth will take the passage literally.

   ---

   [1] Discipleship from *Benson's Creative Bible Studies* by Dennis Benson, Group Books, pp. 357-58.

Bible Study:

1. Gather the class in a circle and read verse 27. Tell the students that they are going to take the words of Jesus seriously.

2. Distribute a broom handle to each student. Have the youth hold the sticks behind their necks, hanging both arms over the ends. They will stand in place for several minutes.

3. While the youth are bearing their "crosses," have each one tell examples of ways he or she feels the pressure of being a Christian. What are the most difficult points of bearing the cross of Christ at school? Work? Home? Among friends? When is it easiest to forget?

4. Ask the students to bend over at the waist with their heads tipped up. Encourage them to do this smoothly and gently for 10 times. They shouldn't strain, but they should physically experience the text. Christ is on the way to the actual cross as He teaches His disciples.

5. Ask the students to set aside the wooden sticks and sit down. There will be sighs of relief from them.

6. Ask the class members how Christ's sacrifice on the cross helps them carry their burdens in everyday life. How does Christ make our burdens light?

7. Give each person several small scraps of paper and a pencil.

8. Ask the youth to imagine that they are going on a trip and they can take only a few of their most important possessions. Have them write the items on separate slips of paper. They can use as many slips as they want. They should not sign their names to the slips.

9. Pass around the piece of cloth and have the students put the slips in it. Tie the bundle and slip it on the end of a mop handle. You now have a primitive knapsack for travel.

10. Read verse 33 and pass around the bundle. Ask each person to take out a slip and read it.

11. Talk about the feelings they get when Jesus offers such an uncompromising teaching. Can they give up what is important for discipleship? What does Jesus really require? How "practical" is following Jesus in our day? Why are our earthly possessions unimportant?

12. Close with a prayer circle asking God for the courage to be His disciples.

Action: Have the students take on an added responsibility of another person this coming week. It must be an intentional task of caring or serving such as volunteering to help an elderly person with his or her shopping. Discuss their experiences at the beginning of the next Bible study.

DISCUSSION STARTERS

1. Do you feel that it is easy or hard to live for Christ? Explain.

2. Is it tough to share your faith with non-Christians? Why or why not?

3. What does the Bible say about suffering?

4. Does suffering reveal a lack of faith or strong faith? Either? Both? None?

5. Why do Christians struggle with peer pressure concerning their faith?

5. The Need for Right-On Attitudes

THE BIG IDEA

People feel that attitudes are important. They are right! We have THE model for right attitudes—our Lord Jesus Christ.

USING THE WORKBOOK

1. Discover what your group believes about attitudes. Find out how they define attitudes.

2. Each person with a Bible should look up the various verses on pages 27-29. Have them read each passage, then open up for dialogue. What do they see in the verses?

3. Move on to Philippians 2:5-11 on page 29. What type of attitudes did Jesus have? What attitudes are we to have?

4. Focus upon the word *humility*. Have someone read Matthew 23:12; James 4:10, and 1 Peter 5:6. Ask them, "What does it mean to be humble?" Then amplify upon the statement, "True humbleness isn't thinking you are a *worm*, but it is knowing who you are in Jesus, and *depending on Him* in every area." Discuss briefly that putting yourself down and degrading yourself is not humility!

5. Help your group finish the statements, "The one thing I learned through this study on attitudes is . . ." and "Now that I know about humility and servanthood, I am (will) . . ."

RELATED SCRIPTURE

Proverbs 15:33   1 Peter 5:5   Colossians 3:12,13
Galatians 5:13

SPECIAL EXPERIENCES

Read John 13:1-17. Give a short talk on servanthood and humility. Read a few commentaries on this passage, or Charles Swindoll's *Improving Your Serve*. Have some water pots filled, and then have each wash another's feet. Make sure there are towels for them to dry off with! Then ask how they felt about washing someone's feet and having their own feet washed. Close in prayer, asking God to help each one grow in humility and servanthood.

DISCUSSION STARTERS

1. How would you define humility?

2. What humble traits did Jesus have?

3. Do you consider yourself to be selfish?

4. What's the difference between attitudes and actions?

5. Name a person who is humble.

6. Walk Your Talk

THE BIG IDEA

God wants us to live what we believe, to practice what we preach. . .to walk our talk!

USING THE WORKBOOK

1. Seek to have the youth explain their understanding of salvation in relation to the verses listed (page 32). Help the group understand that salvation is by grace and is a life-style leading to service. Do not miss the discussion on being a disciple (page 33). What do these verses mean?

2. Encourage each person to learn a memory verse on page 34 under the section "We have our part."

3. Explain that we have our part as Christians and that God has a responsibility, too. God will meet His part; will we? Have the youth talk about Philippians 2:14,15 (page 35).

4. Have them answer the question at the top of page 36, "Do people know I'm a Christian? If so, would they want to know more about Christ because of the way I act?"

5. Complete the Application section. This will help them do a personal inventory of their own spiritual walk with God.

RELATED SCRIPTURE

2 Timothy 2:1-6   Matthew 10:37,38   Matthew 16:24,25
Ephesians 2:5-10

SPECIAL EXPERIENCES

Being a disciple means radical commitment. What will stretch your kids into this level of faith? Ideas: trip downtown to inner city; handing out tracts at a mall; picket a store that sells pornography; take a short-term missions trip; lead a neighborhood kids club; ask to share your faith from the Sunday morning pulpit.

What Do You Say?[1] (Luke 9:18-25)

1. When I compare my own life to the standard laid down in Luke 9:18-25 for a "follower of Jesus," I feel like (*circle one*):
   a. getting involved
   b. erasing my past
   c. rethinking where I am
   d. starting all over again
   e. going for broke
   f. ducking
   g. yawning

2. If Jesus were to ask the same question of me that He asked Peter, "*Who do you say I am?*" I would have to say He is (*circle two*):
   a. my friend
   b. a great teacher
   c. an embarrassment
   d. the Son of God
   e. love
   f. Savior
   g. someone I want to know
   h. a mystery
   i. don't know

3. "*If anyone wants to come with me, he must forget himself, take up his cross every day, and follow me.*" This sounds like (*circle two*):
   a. a commercial
   b. a Sunday school lesson
   c. an appeal for help
   d. something worth giving my life to
   e. getting back to fundamentals
   f. a father-son or mother-daughter talk

---

[1] *What Do You Say?* from *Youth Ministry Encyclopedia*, Serendipity by Lyman Coleman, pp. 156-57.

4. If I could compare my own Christian life to a football game, I would be right now (circle one):

    a. suiting up
    b. waiting for the game to start
    c. sitting on the bench
    d. playing "catch up"
    e. at half time
    f. on the injured list
    g. worn out
    h. giving it all I've got

5. My favorite way of dodging the issue of Christian discipleship is by (circle one):

    a. claiming I don't understand
    b. saying nobody else is serious
    c. just ignoring it
    d. putting it off until next week
    e. asking somebody else to go first

6. My biggest fear in going further in my Christian commitment is the fear of being (circle one):

    a. laughed at by my friends
    b. considered anti-intellectual
    c. cramped in my life-style
    d. a failure
    e. "too" emotional
    f. called a sissy
    g. asked to give up something important

7. If God could deal with me right now like a principal, He would probably (circle two):

    a. chew me out
    b. suspend me
    c. make me stay after school
    d. give me extra work
    e. be patient with my mistakes
    f. put His arm around me and say He is proud of me
    g. give me a swift kick in the pants
    h. put me in charge of something

8. An attitude I need to transfer from athletic training into my spiritual training is *(rank top three 1, 2, 3)*:

____absolute dedication
____knowledge of the game
____team loyalty and support
____day-to-day training
____a good mental attitude
____desire to win
____ability to bounce back from a loss
____long-range strategy
____team spirit
____concentration on the basics

____ _____
____ _____

DISCUSSION STARTERS

1. Have you ever struggled over knowing that you have eternal life?

2. Do you feel you are a disciple after reading verses like Luke 9:23 and Luke 14:25-33?

3. What have you given up for the sake of following Christ?

4. What risky step will you take for Christ?

7.   Finding a Good Friend

THE BIG IDEA

God is interested in us being a good friend to someone plus having a good friend.

USING THE WORKBOOK

1. Read Philippians 2:19-30 out loud. Ask the kids if they have ever heard of Timothy or Epaphroditus before.

2. Why are friendships important? Do you have many friends? How many friends does a person need?

3. Look at the principles on friendships on pages 38 and 39:

    a.   Selfishness kills friendships.
    b.   Commitment builds relationships.

    Ask the youth what these mean.

4. Make sure the group looks up the verses on pages 39 and 40.

RELATED SCRIPTURE

Proverbs 17:17   John 15:12,13   1 Samuel 18:1-4

SPECIAL EXPERIENCES

1. Listen to these two songs and critique them:

    "Friends," from Michael W. Smith Project (Reunion Records, 1982)
    "Friends," by Kenny Marks (Word Incorporated, 1985)

    What do you like about these songs? Agree? Disagree?

2. Have some kids role play a friendship that lacks commitment, one that has commitment, and one that has selfishness as its root.

3. **Caught in the Middle**[1]

   Your English class has gone to the library to work on a research assignment. Several of your friends are goofing around while you are trying to work. One of your friends pulls the fire alarm. The librarian blames you, and you are suspended from school for a day. You don't want to squeal on your friend, but you don't really want to be suspended either.

   What would you do? Give your reason.

   What should you do? Give your reason.

DISCUSSION STARTERS

1. How would you define the word "friend"?

2. List some qualities on a chalkboard that characterize a good friend.

3. How many friends do you have?

4. How do you know if someone will be a true friend to you, plus remain one over the years?

5. Is there a person who only is a friend when he needs you? Have you ever done this to someone?

---

[1] *Caught in the Middle* from *Tension Getters #3*, published by Youth Specialties, p. 21.

8. Getting to Know God

THE BIG IDEA

God's overall goal for His people is to know Him personally. This chapter will give up some clear steps on getting to know God.

USING THE WORKBOOK

1. Dig into Paul's testimony (Philippians 3:4-9) on page 42. Have a discussion based on the fact that Paul was not a wimp. Before becoming a Christian, he was well-established, but coming to Christ was the greatest event in his life.

2. Have the youth focus on the top of page 43: "What are some areas of your life that you are willing to give up for Christ?" Have the youth share out loud or on paper. This will help you as the leader to get a "pulse" on *where* your kids are.

3. Focus on Philippians 3:10: "I want to know Christ and the power of his resurrection and the fellowship of sharing in his sufferings, becoming like him in his death" (NIV). Ask: What does it mean to know God? Why does God want to know us? Why should we know God? Then have the youth list three ways they can know Christ better.

4. Use pages 44 and 45 as practical teaching on getting to know God:

    a. Recognize where you've been.

    b. Be teachable.

    c. Press on for the goal.

    Have them reflect briefly on each section; this will help the kids see where their priorities are.

5. Have the students complete the statements on page 46 to another person in the group:

    a.   Right now, the major goal in my life is . . .

    b.   If I died tonight, I:

        1. am sure that I'd be in heaven.

        2. hope that I'll go to heaven.

        3. have no idea.

RELATED SCRIPTURE

Ephesians 4:12-16   Colossians 1:27,28   Matthew 22:37,38

SPECIAL EXPERIENCES

Give Yourself a Hand![1]

Take an inventory of your life by ranking each statement from 1 to 10 (1 is very low and 10 is very high).

In living out my commitment to Christ

1   2   3   4   5   6   7   8   9   10

In reshaping my life-style around spiritual values

1   2   3   4   5   6   7   8   9   10

In putting my money where my mouth is

1   2   3   4   5   6   7   8   9   10

In developing a daily devotional habit

1   2   3   4   5   6   7   8   9   10

---

[1] Give Yourself a Hand! from *Youth Ministry Encyclopedia*, Serendipity by Lyman Coleman, pp. 186-87.

In keeping thoughts under control

1   2   3   4   5   6   7   8   9   10

In standing up for what I believe

1   2   3   4   5   6   7   8   9   10

In controlling my temper

1   2   3   4   5   6   7   8   9   10

In dealing with family relationships

1   2   3   4   5   6   7   8   9   10

In managing my time for best use

1   2   3   4   5   6   7   8   9   10

In sharing my faith with my friends

1   2   3   4   5   6   7   8   9   10

In working for justice for all peoples

1   2   3   4   5   6   7   8   9   10

In thinking of my long-range goals

1   2   3   4   5   6   7   8   9   10

In experiencing God's inner peace

1   2   3   4   5   6   7   8   9   10

In discovering my own special gifts

1   2   3   4   5   6   7   8   9   10

In dealing with feelings of insecurity and inadequacy

1   2   3   4   5   6   7   8   9   10

In dealing with sexual hangups

1   2   3   4   5   6   7   8   9   10

In experiencing God's forgiveness

1   2   3   4   5   6   7   8   9   10

In believing in myself

1   2   3   4   5   6   7   8   9   10

DISCUSSION STARTERS

1. Do you feel most Americans know God? Explain.

2. Some people know a lot about God. How does knowledge lead us to or hinder us from knowing God?

3. Why is it important to know God? Why does God want us to know Him? Is God lonely?

4. Are you teachable?

5. Is your knowledge of God foggy or clear?

9.   Is There an Afterlife?

THE BIG IDEA

All of us will die. The question is: Where will we spend eternity?

USING THE WORKBOOK

1. Paraphrase Philippians 3:17-21 or read it in a Good News or Living Bible. Ask the students: "What are some common beliefs about the afterlife?" (Examples: No afterlife, soul sleep, all good people go to heaven)

2. Ask: "What do *you* believe about the afterlife?" This will open a "can of worms."

3. What is Paul's dilemma (page 49) in Philippians 3:20,21? Paul wanted to go to heaven and be with Jesus when he died. But he also desired to stay on earth and do more for God's kingdom. You might ask the kids if they are ready to go to heaven now or want to stay here longer. Probe deeply.

4. Talk about page 50 and the changes that will be made upon our own resurrection. Kids love to hear that our bodies and lives will be changed. You might want to talk about Revelation chapters 20, 21, and 22.

5. Review page 51 on the three pointers concerning the afterlife. These pointers are vital, especially if any students have not made a commitment to Christ.

RELATED SCRIPTURE

Revelation 20   Revelation 21   Revelation 22
Romans 3   Romans 6   Romans 10:9,10

SPECIAL EXPERIENCES

1. Take your kids through the *Four Spiritual Laws* or *Peace with God* booklets, and lead them in prayer to receive Christ (if they have not already). It's a goal to share one's faith.

2. Use the *Assurance of Salvation* booklet (Navigators) to show Scriptural promises on assurance of salvation.

3. Go with the students to a cemetery for a visual-aid effect. See how many gravestone inscriptions deal with the afterlife.

4. Die and come back to life to tell us about it! (Just kidding!)

5. Attend a nursing home or hospital cancer ward and ask the patients about their joys and fears of death, dying, and the afterlife.

DISCUSSION STARTERS

1. Are you fearful of death?

2. Do you have any doubts about your being in heaven?

3. What scares you most about dying?

4. What do you think heaven will be like?

5. Have you ever had a close encounter with death? What were your feelings?

10. Guidelines for Dynamic Living

THE BIG IDEA

Do you want to be a dull, boring Christian? God has big plans for us to have a dynamic, exciting life in Christ.

USING THE WORKBOOK

The opening sentence needs to be stated: "God wants our lives to be dynamic!" Probably your members face boredom. This lesson is to help kids rise above mediocrity.

1. Spend some time working on the chart (page 53). Have the group memorize Philippians 4:4 and 4:6.

2. Go over the five principles on growing into a dynamic Christian (pages 54-57). Major on the questions under *Rejoice in the Lord* (page 54).

   Ask the kids, "of the five principles, which is the easiest and which the most difficult to practice?" Let them share their "confessions."

3. Probe into principle four on pages 55 and 56. Do the "What goes into your mind" fill-ins. This reveals what the kids are doing with their thought life.

4. Encourage the young people to complete page 57. Have them be specific and practical.

RELATED SCRIPTURE

1 Thessalonians 5:16-18   John 14:12-15

SPECIAL EXPERIENCES

1. Go interview another church's youth leaders and group members. Ask them, "What does it mean to be a dynamic Christian and how does one grow into a dynamic believer?"

2. Out of the five principles, have the students pick one area that they need to work on. They should set a goal. Example: "Rejoice in the Lord." I will rejoice and thank God each morning as I rise from my bed for the next two weeks."

3. Pull out some Bible concordances and have the youth find out what the Bible says about these words: rejoice, joy, worry (anxious), and pray. This teaches the youth how to cross-reference passages.

DISCUSSION STARTERS

1. Do you consider yourself a vibrant, exciting Christian?

2. Do you know someone who lives a dynamic Christian life?

3. What ingredients/characteristics are needed to live 100 percent for Christ?

4. Do you worry much?

5. Do you grumble and complain often?

6. How much music do you listen to? TV?

11. Having the Right Stuff

THE BIG IDEA

Life can be tough. With the right ingredients, we will keep on growing spiritually.

USING THE WORKBOOK

Read through Philippians 4:10-23. Have the kids define commitment. There are four commitments we want them to "go for."

1. Most youth who make a commitment to anything are looking for some benefit, promise, or reward. There are two major promises in this passage of Scripture. This first is *Christ's strength* (verse 13) and the second is *Christ's provision* (verse 19).

   Ask the students: "In order to receive these promises, what do we need to do?" Verses 10-23 explain.

   a. Learn contentment.

   b. Look to the power source.

   c. Be a giver.

   d. Get close to Christians.

2. Encourage them to make a wholehearted commitment to the four principles above.

3. Ask your group, "How does one learn to be content?" One answer might be "through prayer" or "get close to Christians."

4. Stress to the youth that the Bible commands us to be involved with other Christians. Help them avoid the "Lone Ranger" mentality.

Reiterate the need to get close to believers. "Do you have a close Christian friend? If not, find one!"

5. Memorize either Philippians 4:13 or 4:19 as a group. Urge the youth to renew their minds with these verses when tempted. There is power in God's Word. Faith is believing God's Word (see Mark 11:22-24; Romans 10:17). When feeling defeated, the youth can say, "Lord, I feel weak or insecure, but I stand on Your promise in Philippians 4:13 that 'I can do all things through him who strengthens me.' "

RELATED SCRIPTURE

Psalm 42:1,2   2 Corinthians 8   2 Corinthians 9

SPECIAL EXPERIENCES

Ideas for Social Action[1]

1. Service projects produce a sense of giving, contentment, and closeness to God and those Christians with whom you work. Try one of the suggested projects below.

A Cup of Cool Water in His Name

Here's a service project for those hot summer days. Have the youth group borrow or rent some large coolers (the kind that have a little spout on them) and fill them with fresh water. Then, go to places where there are lots of thirsty people and offer free cups of water. This could be done at the beach, or on a street corner, or in a shopping mall, or anywhere. The cooler could be pulled along in a wagon, a guy could carry it on a backpack frame, or you could set up a table with the cooler and cups on it so that people could just help themselves. A sign on the table or on the cooler could let people know that this is a service of your youth group— in response to the "living water" that Jesus gives.

Easter Baskets

A good project for Easter would be to obtain some Easter baskets and

---

[1] From *Ideas for Social Action* by Anthony Campolo, published by Youth Specialties, pp. 49-50 and 66-69.

fill them with colored eggs and other goodies that could be distributed to underprivileged children. There are children in orphanages, retarded children's homes, hospitals, missions, and poor neighborhoods who never enjoy this aspect of the Easter celebration. Perhaps a group could deliver the baskets and share with the children the story of Easter in word and song.

Easter Caroling

Everyone goes caroling at Christmas, so why not at Easter as well? You can go caroling at private homes or you can go caroling at institutions (like convalescent hospitals). If you do go to institutions, be sure to contact them first and let them know what you want to do. It may take a little extra "explaining." Meet an hour or so early to make sure that everyone knows the songs you will be singing. Choose songs of joy that effectively communicate the Easter message. You may want to choose songs that are familiar enough that those being sung to can join in and sing along. Your pastor can come and administer communion to the shut-ins and others if you think it would be appropriate. Another good idea is to get some flowers ahead of time and to present Easter bouquets to those to whom you sing. You will find that because it's so unexpected, caroling at Easter will go even better than Christmas caroling. Start a new tradition!

Free Car Wash

This one usually blows everybody's mind. Have your youth group organize a regular car wash (at a gas station, shopping center, or the church parking lot) but instead of selling tickets, have the kids give them away. You may want to make it clear that there are "no strings attached." It really is a "Free Car Wash." You might want to notify the news media ahead of time and ask them to run a story in advance letting people know that this is not just a gimmick, or another way to get people's money. The idea behind the car wash is that it is a free gift from the youth group to the community—a gesture of Christian love and friendship.

You can, of course, accept donations if you want to, but this should not be emphasized if you want to make it a true act of service. You might want to do this on a Saturday and then discuss what happened (the reactions of people, etc.) with your youth group on Sunday.

Servant Week

This is a summer activity that could be done in addition to or in place of a normal summer camp. It requires a full week, and it could be done like a "lock-in" where the kids camp out for a week inside the church. The emphasis of the week is "servanthood," with the first part of the week (a day or so) spent doing some Bible study on the subject. Kids need to know how important the concept of serving others is to the Christian life.

The rest of the week is spent actually doing service projects. One day can be spent working around the church, another can be spent visiting or working in a convalescent home, another day can be spent putting on a children's program, etc. Each day should be different with a different emphasis. The kids can discuss the experiences of each day in the evening back at the camp.

Something like this will take a lot of advance preparation, but the rewards are great. You will find that your young people will have their lives affected much more profoundly by a week of serving others than by going away for a week of fun and inspiration at summer camp.

Sponsor a Child

There are many agencies like World Vision and Holt International which try to find financial sponsors for children in orphanages overseas. Usually these agencies will ask for a certain amount of money to provide food, clothing, and shelter for particular children each month. Most of the time you can select a child to sponsor by name and receive detailed information about the child, including photos, and sometimes handwritten thank-you notes from the child.

Why not ask your church group to "adopt" one of these children and pledge to support the child on a monthly basis? Each person in the youth group can give a certain amount, like $1.00 per month, and the child's progress can be monitored by the entire group. The group will know the child's name and will really feel involved in that child's life. The group can also pray for the child on a regular basis. Not only is a project like this easy to do, it helps young people to develop a world awareness and a sense of compassion for others.

Stay-at-Home Work Camp

Most work camps are done at a far-away location—like Mexico, an Indian reservation, or an Appalachian village—but they don't have to be. You can have a work camp right at home.

Find a place in or out of town where your group can sleep and eat during the whole period of the work camp (four to seven days). The kids do need to be away from their homes during the work camp, if possible. Then, find projects nearby that need to be done. These can include painting, remodeling, fixing roofs, clean-up work, weeding, and all sorts of jobs for people who can't afford to have it done themselves.

The only real disadvantage of this (compared to a work camp that is far away) is that there may be unwanted distractions. This is something you would have to deal with. But the advantages are many. You will be able to accomplish more with less expense, you will probably be able to involve more kids, and you will be able to have an impact on your immediate community. It is also much easier to plan and to do follow-up work. Of course the important thing is not whether you do a work camp at home or abroad. The main thing is just to do one. The results will always be worth the effort.

Summer Jamboree

Have your high school or college-age youth conduct a Vacation Bible School during the summer for an inner-city neighborhood. There are usually hundreds of children in these areas who have nothing to do except to play in the streets. A "V.B.S." can be done in cooperation with an inner-city church that hasn't the staff to put one on themselves, or you can simply rent a community hall, use a public park or some other location. You might call it Summer Jamboree, or any other name you choose.

The best way to prepare for this would be to involve your young people in a normal Vacation Bible School at your own church. Usually high schoolers aren't too excited about V.B.S., but if they know that they are going to be putting one on themselves the following week they will take an active role in the first one just to learn.

Advertise your Summer Jamboree throughout the neighborhood. The program itself can consist of the usual things—games, Bible stories puppets, crafts, singing, refreshments, and so on. It can last one or two weeks, mornings or afternoons. Have one day when you invite the parents to come see the activities and a program put on by the kids. Several churches have done this and the results have been tremendous.

Thank You, Officer

Believe it or not, most police officers and others in law enforcement are NOT brutal, tough, impersonal, or corrupt. In fact, the majority of them are average people who have families and friends and who have chosen a profession that puts their lives in great danger while helping others. Rarely do they receive thanks from the public. Mostly they get bad press.

So, why not suggest to your youth group that they do something nice for the cops in town. Maybe you can have a lock-in at the church that begins around 6:00 P.M. Spend the first few hours making a big banner that says something like, "Thanks for a job well done!" Make some cookies, brownies, cupcakes, etc., and then hit the police station around midnight (when they usually change shifts). This should be prearranged with the police department, of course. Put up the banner and pass out the goodies to all the officers who are either coming or going. You'll find that many of them will be genuinely moved by this and will want to stay and talk to your young people for a long time. It's a great way to share the love of Christ with people who don't see very much of it on the job. This can also be done for firemen and other public employees.

2. Make up skits that carry the themes of:

- Contentment

- Giving

- Looking to the Power Source

- Getting Close to Christians

DISCUSSION STARTERS

1. What is contentment? How does a person be content?

2. Why is it so difficult to be content?

3. Why do Christians face pressures?

4. What are the benefits of trusting God?

5. Should we be givers or takers?

12. Pulling It Together

THE BIG IDEA

To sum up the themes of Philippians and to encourage students to get into God's Word on an individual level as well as a corporate one.

USING THE WORKBOOK

1. Each person should be given 20 minutes to give four chapter titles to Philippians (page 63). Then have each person present them to the group.

2. Have each student complete number 2 on page 64: "Sum up what Philippians has meant to you personally. The most meaningful lesson for me was . . ."

3. Have them give an example of number 6 "who" questions.

4. To renew their attention spans, ask someone to explain observation, interpretation, and application in a sentence.

5. Call them to a commitment to personal Bible study.

RELATED SCRIPTURE

Galatians   Ephesians   Colossians
1 John

SPECIAL EXPERIENCES

1. Have each member share his/her favorite verse of Philippians.

2. Ask those who memorized verses to attempt reciting them.

3. Choose what you believe to be the main theme of Philippians (i.e. rejoicing, knowing God) and have each person or small group do a collage on it (pass out magazines, scissors, tape, etc.)

DISCUSSION STARTERS

1. What did you think about our studying Philippians in *Getting It Together*?

2. What major insight did you gain?

3. Do you believe now that Bible study can be fun and exciting?

4. What are your goals for your future in studying the Bible?

5. Would you enjoy doing another study together?

Section 4

Building Relationships...with God and Others

Contents

Introduction

A relationship with God is by far the most valuable journey any person can ever take. The path has been traveled by the many people recorded in the Old and New Testaments. BUILDING A RELATIONSHIP. . .WITH GOD AND OTHERS takes a look at Psalms 120-134, otherwise known as the Songs of Ascent. These 15 psalms received the Songs of Ascent title because the Hebrew people sang them while traveling up to Jerusalem for the various feasts of the year.

The Songs of Ascent were to the Hebrews what a car stereo or Walkman is to many of us today—accompaniment for our long travels. The Hebrews did sing the Songs of Ascent for passing time on a long trip through the hills, valleys, and deserts of the Middle East. Their importance surpassed mere musical entertainment. The words and songs carry the history and heart of the Hebrew faith and love for God.

A few themes run through the entire collection of Psalms 120-134. The most important is the centering of life on God. A second theme is the value of relationships with others. Combine these two themes and you come up with a third theme: obedience and commitment in the midst of life's demands.

A thorough study of these 15 psalmic gems grants the Bible student a discovery of historical Jewish life, refreshing spiritual challenge, and the continual reminder of God's active and loving presence from history to today. Each reader's level of appreciation will increase with his or her understanding of the Hebrew culture and faith. The novice will also discover new and helpful insights about God, others, and life by studying the Songs of Ascent. A helpful reference book for studying the Songs of Ascent is *A Long Obedience in the Same Direction* by Eugene H. Peterson (Inter-Varsity Press, 1980). Books on the Old Testament, Psalms, and Hebrew culture will enhance the preparation of the following workbook chapters.

1. Building a Firm Foundation
Psalm 120,121

THE BIG IDEA

A relationship with God is the strong foundation enabling Christians to live through the hills and valleys of life.

USING THE WORKBOOK

1. The Three Little Pigs story is a famous and familiar story. Use it as a focal point to begin the chapter's theme of building a firm foundation.

2. Read Psalm 121 and relate it to the main principle found in the Three Little Pigs story. Notice the similiar ideas found in verses 1, 6, and 7. Find some examples from the group where God provided protection in a time of trouble.

3. The goal: to build a firm foundation. Paraphrasing Matthew 7:24-27 can be a valuable way for the group to better relate to the words of Jesus.

4. The Lord watches over you. Draw out the picture portrayed in verses 4-6 in Psalm 121. The pictures of shade, sleep, sun, etc. are vivid analogies to help us understand God's protection. Remember that the original psalmists wrote these words while traveling to Jerusalem, not by plane or car, but by animal or on foot.

5. Psalm 120 is inserted as a support to the idea of God's protection in a time of need. Historical background on Meshech and Kedar (verse 5) is helpful for understanding the thinking of the psalmist. They refer to the Gentile peoples among whom the Hebrews lived. Genesis 10:2 and 25:13 mention both names. The psalm's main point is the cry to God for His deliverance.

RELATED SCRIPTURE

Jeremiah 3:23   1 Kings 18:17-39   Isaiah 25:4
Isaiah 49:10   Deuteronomy 28:6   Proverbs 12:21

SPECIAL EXPERIENCES

$3 Worth of God[1]

Read this quote and ask the group how it relates to the pilgrimage of a Christian.

> I'd like to buy $3 worth of God, please, not enough to explode my soul or disturb my sleep, but just enough to equal a cup of warm milk or a snooze in the sunshine. I don't want enough of Him to make me love a black man or pick beets with a migrant. I want ecstasy, not a transformation; I want the warmth of the womb, not a new birth. I want a pound of the Eternal in a paper sack. I would like to buy $3 worth of God, please.

Read Mark 13:32-42 and ask the following questions:

1. What was Jesus' request in verse 34?

2. What did the disciples do?

3. What feelings do you think ran through Jesus when He returned three times only to find His closest friends asleep?

DISCUSSION STARTERS

1. What comes to mind when you hear this statement: "To be a Christian is not easy, but it is not alone"?

2. What keeps us from getting back up or calling on God when we are knocked down?

---

[1] "$3 Worth of God" by Wilbur Rees from *When I Relax I Feel Guilty* by Tim Hansel (Elgin, IL: David C. Cook Publishing Co., 1979), p. 49.

3. Finish this sentence in relation to your life right now: "When the going gets tough . . ."

4. What areas tend to heat up your life thermometer? (peer pressure, family conflicts, irresponsibility, poor self-image, etc.)

5. What do most people choose as the foundation for their lives?

2. Understanding and Enjoying Worship
Psalm 122

THE BIG IDEA

Worshiping God brings a pleasant peace into life.

USING THE WORKBOOK

1. Psalm 122 hits the nail on the head in regard to many worship experiences being boring, especially to youth. Use the opening words to get the group thinking about their worship experiences and expectations.

2. The Pursuit of Worship—Three main points emphasize the importance of the believers participation in worship. Worship is not passive but active. Attitude, praise, and prayer play a big role in the outcome and enjoyment of a believer's worship experience. The philosopher's quote can be a catalyst for a discussion of the pursuit of worship.

3. The Product of Worship—Actively pursuing worship has a direct influence on a believer's life. Discuss the meaning and experience of peace. Contrast the peace received from the world and the peace received from Jesus as mentioned in John 14:27.

4. The Peace Inventory can be a helpful way to look at life. Point out that the areas lacking peace can change because worshiping God promises peace.

5. The final experiment makes for an easy index card handout to carry in a Bible ready for the next worship experience. Use the card as a reminder of God's desire from us during worship.

RELATED SCRIPTURE

Ecclesiastes 4:7-12   Psalm 48:12-14   Psalm 85:10
Ecclesiastes 5:1   Psalm 29:11

SPECIAL EXPERIENCES

1. Many people make excuses for not going to church. Come equipped with a board or large pad and felt-tip pen. Ask the group to list the 20 best excuses for not going to church. For example, "I had a late night last night or "Sunday is my only morning to sleep in."

2. **Creative Worship.** Change the worship experience to eliminate the opportunity for boredom. A few ideas include:

   * Youth Sunday—The entire service planned by the youth group.
   * Creative Worship—Use drama, dance, film, or slides in the service.
   * Modernize the hymns—Write popular hymns to contemporary music.
   * Silent Worship—Use mime and nonverbal communication for a service.
   * Location Worship—Go to a different spot for a special worship service.
   * Candlelight Worship—Use only candles for lighting.
   * Communion—Implement a communion service at your next camp or special event.

DISCUSSION STARTERS

1. What makes most worship experiences boring or meaningless?

2. What could you do to improve the value of your church's worship service?

3. Why is peace a direct result of worship?

4. Have you ever had an experience where you felt very sure of God's presence?

5. Have you ever participated in a worship experience? What made it good?

3. Mercy: God's Style
Psalms 123, 124

THE BIG IDEA

Mercy is God's love and forgiveness in response to our cries. Receiving mercy is the experience that causes a person to become merciful.

USING THE WORKBOOK

1. Read Psalm 123 a few times. Compare the words of the psalmist to the words of David in 2 Samuel 11. The story of David and Bathsheba has enough modern relevance to seize the attention of the group. Use the questions in the workbook to dialogue on the story.

2. **Mercy in Action**—Compare the incident in Matthew 17 to Psalm 124. Try and change the words of Psalm 124 to fit the incident with Jesus. The section ends with an encouragement to list the times when the Lord has shown mercy to us. No doubt a few examples or stories will prove that God is merciful to people today.

3. **Mercy: Your Style**—*The Big Idea* stresses the importance of mercy becoming a life-style as a direct result of receiving mercy. This last section in the chapter shows the call of a Christian to be merciful (Matthew 5:7). Close with the story about Francis of Assisi and his experience with the leper.

RELATED SCRIPTURE

Matthew 25:31-46   Proverbs 14:31   Matthew 4:24
Deuteronomy 4:31   2 Chronicles 30:9   Psalm 136

SPECIAL EXPERIENCES

1. **Modern Day David and Bathsheba**—Have the group list the movies, TV shows, or stories that feature a plot with the same situation as David

and Bathsheba. Discuss the difference between David and the modern characters. What brought David back to God? Why would David seek God's mercy? What keeps people today from seeking God's mercy? What role can we take as merciful people to help others experience God's mercy?

2. **Love a Loner**—Have the group members think of various persons they have encountered who appear to be loners much like the leper in the Francis of Assisi story. Plan action steps of mercy toward these people. Is it a local street person? How about a loner on campus? Does anyone work with a neglected person? Would they come to the next group meeting?

DISCUSSION STARTERS

1. What keeps us from being merciful people?

2. Why would Jesus make mercy one of the Beatitudes?

3. How did David feel after he was confronted by Nathan?

4. How did David feel after receiving God's mercy?

5. How do you feel when someone expresses mercy to you in a time of loneliness?

4. Becoming A Person of Integrity
Psalm 125

THE BIG IDEA

Being a Christian with integrity is a description of a person who is committed to Christ in both words and actions, not just in words. Their hearts are "upright" and their actions seek good.

USING THE WORKBOOK

1. A geographical background on Jerusalem will help the group understand the reference to Mount Zion and Jerusalem. Consider using a map of the Middle East and a dictionary or encyclopedia description of the geography surrounding the city of Jerusalem. The leader could pass out the maps and books and have the group members do research to better understand the psalm.

2. The Requirement—Trust is the main point for the first section. A person of integrity is one who places all of his or her trust in the Lord. Such trust provides the confidence to live out a life of integrity in spite of the circumstances.

3. The Risk—Living for God can be a risky business. Verse 3 emphasizes the protection of God, but the Bible is full of accounts portraying the risk of following God. Use the risk scale to stimulate discussion of each person's choice to step out and risk.

4. The Result—The third part of integrity is the reward God delivers for those who stand for Him. The phrase "upright in their hearts" (RSV) in verse 4 is the Bible's description of integrity. Contrast it with the result of lack of integrity mentioned in verse 5.

5. Integrity is a lifestyle of commitment. The chapter finishes with two

areas of commitment for a believer: a commitment to trust and a commitment to truth.

Strive to help the group see beyond the cost of commitment to the treasure of integrity mentioned in Proverbs 2:7. Discuss examples of disaster that happened to people that might be the result of lack of integrity and lack of protection from God. The closing section refers to John 14:6 and Jesus' claim to be the Truth. Help the group to see that a commitment to truth is in actuality a commitment to Jesus Christ.

RELATED SCRIPTURE

Job 2:9,10   Psalm 18:30   Psalm 41:12
Proverbs 14:32   Proverbs 19:1   Proverbs 20:7
John 11:25   John 10:9

SPECIAL EXPERIENCES

What would you do if . . .

1. You're sitting at a red light in the left turn lane. Three minutes pass and there is no change in the light. Would you . . .
    a. Look for police or oncoming cars and go?
    b. Turn right, drive to the nearest left turn, make a U-turn?
    c. Wait for the light to change?
    d. Other.

2. You leave a store and drive halfway home before you realize the clerk overpaid you. Would you . . .

    a. Say "Next time I'll pay it back"?
    b. Thank God for the financial blessing?
    c. Turn around and return the money?
    d. Other.

3. You are asked to close the store at which you work. The store closes at 10 P.M., but from 8-9:30 P.M. no patrons come to the store. At 9:30 would you . . .

    a. Close the store early and save the owner money (electricity, pay, etc.)?
    b. Wait until 10 P.M. to close?
    c. Call the owner and ask for permission?
    d. Other.

4. The person of your dreams says yes to your request for a date. At the time you are dating someone else. Would you . . .

   a. Go on the date and then break up with your present date?
   b. Call your present date and call it quits before the date?
   c. Go on the date and quit calling your present date?
   d. Other.

Create your own situations.

DISCUSSION STARTERS

1. Why is it difficult to trust in the Lord?

2. What makes someone more risky than another?

3. Who is your best example of a person of integrity?

4. Does lying ever become good or purposeful? When?

5. If integrity was a crime, do you possess enough of it to be arrested?

5. Laughter: Joy-filled Living
Psalm 126

THE BIG IDEA

A relationship with God is the fertile ground for a life filled with true joy and laughter.

USING THE WORKBOOK

1. The beginning is almost too serious for a discussion of laughter. The idea is to bring to mind the many things that cause a chuckle, giggle, or deep roar of laughter. If the introduction is creative and funny, you will be more successful in making your point.

2. Today's Joy—The first section takes a close look at the joyful lives of the Hebrew people and their influence on other people. Discuss the influence of joyful people on lives of the group members. Use Nehemiah 8:10 for a great memory verse. Take a few moments to reflect on the Lord's great work in the lives of each group member. Stress the goodness of God that brings about joy. (The watercourses of Negev as mentioned in verse 4 refer to a desert area that became ablaze with blossoms after a rain.)

3. Tomorrow's Joy—Now the chapter becomes a fun and practical way to bring refreshment to others. Isaiah 35:5-7 is a beautiful picture of the life God brings. Move your group toward practical ways to spread joy around their circles of friends, family, and strangers.

RELATED SCRIPTURE

Philippians 4:4,5   Romans 12:12   Deuteronomy 26:5-9
Exodus 15:1,2   John 15:11   Luke 2:8-14

SPECIAL EXPERIENCES

1. **To Tell the Truth**

   A fun game to get a group laughing at some very funny experiences. Break the group into teams of four people. Have each of the teams pick one true "most embarassing story" from one of their team members' lives. Have each team write down their one story. The entire group gathers back together to play the game. The leader picks one team at a time to line up in front of the group. The leader reads this team's embarrassing story. The rest of the group has three minutes or 20 questions to try and guess who was the real culprit in the story. The object of the team up front is to stump the rest of the group. Therefore, each of the team members up front needs to make it sound like they were the one in the story. After the allotted time, the group is asked to vote for who they think is the real owner of the story. The team who fooled the most people is the winning team.

2. **Creating Joy in Others**[1]

   There are plenty of ways to bring fun, creative, and joyful experiences into others' lives. Here are a few ideas:

   a. Hide a quarter in your little sister's clothing drawer every week.

   b. Secretly add a few gallons of gas to your parents' car every day.

   c. Sneak into your parents' closet and shine all the shoes.

   d. Get your group to spell out "Happy Mother's Day" on a grass lawn, take pictures of it, and sent it to Mom.

   e. Borrow your parents' car and take it to a friend's house and wash and wax it. Do the same for your friend's car at your house.

   f. Put a fake phone in your car, locker, or book bag. Make phone calls on it in a traffic jam, between classes, or during an English final. If a teacher sees you in the class, hand her the receiver and say, "it's for you."

   ---

   [1] *Creating Joy in Others* © from the 1986 *Grow For It* magazine, published by Youth Specialties, pp. 30,31.

g. Write encouraging notes to family and friends and tape them to notebooks, toothbrushes, math books, windshields, and celery stalks in the refrigerator.

DISCUSSION STARTERS

1. What is the funnist story or joke you have ever heard?

2. What enables Christians to be joyful in spite of circumstances?

3. Jerry Lewis, the comedian/actor, has a motto in his dressing room. It says, "There are three things that are real: God, human folly, and laughter. Since the first two are beyond our comprehension, we must do what we can with the third." (Quoted in *Living on the Ragged Edge* by Charles Swindoll [Waco, TX: Word, Inc., 1985], p. 44). What do you think about this motto?

4. Why do some people remain so sad and miserable?

5. When was the last time you had a good laugh? What made you do so?

6. Successful Living
Psalm 127

THE BIG IDEA

Successful living comes as a result of putting God first.

USING THE WORKBOOK

Two areas of life are evaluated in Psalm 127: Success in the world and success at home.

1. Success in the World—Read Psalm 127:1,2 and use it as a description of the vanity or uselessness of living and working without God. The section refers to Matthew 6:25-32, an accurate description of our worry-filled world. Discuss what it means to seek first the kingdom of God as mentioned in Matthew 6:33.

2. Success at Home—Psalm 127:3-5 portrays the successful living found in a godly home. Discuss the value of the biblical insight found in the three Proverbs references in this section.

3. Make Matthew 6:33 a memory verse for the group.

RELATED SCRIPTURE

2 Thessalonians 3:11-13   Genesis 11:1-9   Matthew 19:28
Luke 18:29,30

SPECIAL EXPERIENCES

1. **What's Number One?**[1]

These questions are to be answered by each individual on a sheet of paper, then followed by a discussion:

a. What's your favorite magazine?

b. If you could be anyone else, who would you be?

c. When you daydream, what are you doing?

d. If you could buy anything, what would you buy?

e. When you picture yourself doing something "cool and neat" (mental act of heroism), what are you doing?

f. What would you like to do for your life's work?

g. What's good about you? (Don't be humble.)

Relate the above questions to Matthew 6:33.

2. Compare and contrast Psalm 127 with the story of the Tower of Babel in Genesis 11:1-9.

DISCUSSION STARTERS

1. How do you define success?

2. How does God define success?

3. How does the world define success?

4. What makes people worry?

5. What area of your life causes you to worry more than other areas?

6. How do you define vanity?

---

[1] *What's Number One?* © from *Ideas 9-12*, published by Youth Specialties, p. 110.

7. Living a Happy Life
Psalm 128

THE BIG IDEA

Happiness is the result of fearing the Lord.

USING THE WORKBOOK

This psalm is thought by many to have been sung at Israelite marriage ceremonies. Family happiness is dependent upon the blessing of God.

1. Happiness is the center of many pursuits in life. Use the beginning survey to introduce a discussion of happiness. After allowing the group to define happiness, compare different views.

2. Psalm 128 is clearly divided into three sections:

   Happiness of an individual and his or her relationship with God. Fear of the Lord is the main theme for the psalm. The workbook chapter refers to Proverbs 1:7 where again the fear of the Lord is the prerequisite for the entire wisdom of Proverbs. Make sure the group understands the full Hebrew meaning of "fear" which is unlike our modern definition.

   Two steps arise from the first verse. These steps of attitude and action are plugged in again in the next two sections.

   Happiness in my family. The psalm speaks again of the blessedness of family for a man who fears the Lord. The "color of the family" exercise is a less threatening way for group members to speak honestly about the good and bad of family situations. The same two steps of attitude and action are used again, this time in the family context. The evaluation tool is a tangible way to summarize the family situation. Many people feel hopeless when it comes to their family. Provide hope with the psalm.

Happiness in my world. The two steps are used again, attitude and action. Two steps are simple to remember but challenging to use. Encourage the group to develop a habit of asking. "What is my attitude?" and "What is my Action?"

RELATED SCRIPTURE

Ecclesiastes 12:13   Matthew 5:1-11   Micah 6:8
Genesis 12:2   Psalm 34:8   Psalm 144:15
Psalm 146:5   Proverbs 8:32

SPECIAL EXPERIENCES

1. Use the first few questions for a community survey. Go to a surrounding neighborhood and ask:

    a. What are you looking for in life?

    b. What is happiness?

    c. What makes you happy?

2. Read Genesis 12 and discuss the *attitude* and *action* Abraham took in response to God's promise of a blessing. Include the family and national elements of Abraham's life.

DISCUSSION STARTERS

1. In your opinion, how many people out of every 100 are truly happy?

2. What comes to mind when you think of the word "fear"?

3. Why are families so unhappy?

4. What do you think when you hear that the family is the most violent place in our nation?

5. What will it take to turn our nation back to "fearing the Lord"?

8. Faithfulness: Hanging in There

Psalm 129

THE BIG IDEA

Throughout the history of the Old Testament, God never left nor forsook His people.

USING THE WORKBOOK

1. A good understanding of Old Testament history will provide the group with a better appreciation for the affliction suffered by the Hebrew people. A possible brief summary could include the captivity in Egypt (Exodus 1:8-14) and Babylon (2 Chronicles 36:15-21). Emphasize the triumph of the Israelites as mentioned in Psalm 129:2.

2. The Danger Zone—This section discusses the troubles of Paul as a result of obedience, not disobedience. Christians should never be deceived with the idea of Christianity equaling constant pleasure. Discuss Paul's experience with danger. Stimulate a clarification of tough times as a result of disobedience and tough times due to obedience.

3. The Victory Zone—The Hebrew people and Paul both experienced the righteousness of the Lord. Victory is sweet but seldom easy. This section focuses on hope without losing sight of the long journey.

4. Hebrews 12:1,2 is the summary verse that pulls together the entire psalm. The Hebrews 12 Scripture refers to the surrounding witnesses mentioned in Hebrews 11. The Hall of Faith in chapter 11 is a consistent reference to Old Testament times like Psalm 129.

RELATED SCRIPTURE

Psalm 119:137-144   Matthew 16:18   1 Corinthians 9:24-27
Philippians 4:13

SPECIAL EXPERIENCES

1. Divide up the various characters in Hebrews 11. Assign one character or group of characters to a small group. Have them become research reporters who look up the Hebrew 11 persons in their Old Testament. Then have each group report back to the group at large.

2. Take the group to a local jail and discuss the experience of being locked up. What would it be like to be held in captivity? How would you feel?

DISCUSSION STARTERS

1. Do modern Christians in highly developed countries lack the stick-to-itiveness possessed by the Israelites?

2. How do you think the Israelites felt while in captivity?

3. Why do many people choose disobedience over obedience to God?

4. Is your life surrounded by danger zones? What is the cost for a change of danger zones? (Example: changing or losing friends because of negative influences)

5. How do you think Paul felt when God did not remove the thorn in the flesh?

6. What sins cling close to you?

9. Understanding Prayer
Psalm 130

THE BIG IDEA

Prayer is the task of waiting confidently on God for His answer.

USING THE WORKBOOK

1. **The Goal of Prayer**. The goal of prayer is defined in this section as turning to the right source for help. Part of the turning process includes the confession of sin or iniquity as mentioned in Psalm 130:3. The goal is to draw people before God in a confessing state of prayer. Knowing that God forgives and forgets is the transforming good news discovered in prayer. Each member should draw one key point out of the first four verses of Psalm 130: "God will forgive me."

2. **The Growth in Prayer**. Once forgiveness is received, we're ready for action. "Let's go, Lord" we say. Yet, the psalmist waits and waits and waits. Waiting is not wasting. Waiting is concentrating all effort and resources in expectation of the arrival. Help the group to understand that waiting on God communicates our trust in Him. If God is God, why not let Him take charge? Isaiah 40:30,31 are encouraging words for those who wait. Waiting is growing.

3. **The Gift of Prayer**. Hope is the most obvious difference between a Christian and a non-Christian. Hope as defined in the workbook is the experience in the past that lends confidence to the future. The Moses story in Exodus 14:21-29 was a vivid reminder to the Hebrew people of God's plans for them. The group will gain hope as they develop a thankful heart. Christians have hope because they have strong memories of the life, death, and resurrection of Jesus Christ.

4. **Prayer is learned by practice**. Try to make prayer a significant part of every gathering. It often becomes a ritual of opening and closing, not vital communication with God. Plan ahead for extra time to write out the prayers.

RELATED SCRIPTURE

John 17:1-26   Matthew 26:36-44   Psalm 3:3,4
Matthew 6:5-15   Psalm 4:1   Psalm 51:2

SPECIAL EXPERIENCES

1. Start a group prayer notebook. Use it as a hope-building reminder of God's active hand in our lives.

2. Purchase journals for each member of the group. The journals can be simple notebooks all the way up to published journals like the *Grow For It* journal by Youth Specialties.

3. Study prayers in the Bible.

4. Study prayer life-styles of biblical persons.

DISCUSSION STARTERS

1. Why can prayer be difficult to practice?

2. What keeps us from accepting forgiveness?

3. Why is waiting so tough?

4. Finish this sentence, "I hope . . ."

5. Prayer is to spiritual growth like _____ is to _____.

10. Humility: A Trademark of Walking with God
Psalm 131

THE BIG IDEA

The Lord grants hope to the humble.

USING THE WORKBOOK

1. Begin the chapter with a look back at the fun years of childhood. Try to get group members to remember their positive experiences. The message of Psalm 131 is to remain humbled and quiet before our Lord like a child before his or her parent.

2. The Problem of Pride—Pride is the major problem between people and God. Paraphrasing verse 1 will help each person to understand the psalmist David's true attitude. The section takes a thorough look at the Tower of Babel story in contrast to Psalm 131. Paint the picture of the two attitudes of pride and humility. Emphasize the consequences mentioned at the end of the section: Pride = Problems but Humility = Hope.

3. The Hope of Humility—The analogy of a child and its mother is a vivid picture of humble dependence. Refer to Matthew 18:1-3 to gain Jesus' high view of a childlike dependence. The exercise of thinking back to childhood can be a very affirming experience. Stress the importance placed on childlike qualities in God's kingdom. Affirm those in the group who still possess a high percentage of childlike qualities.

RELATED SCRIPTURE

Mark 10:13-16

Hebrews 5:12,13

James 4:6

1 Peter 2:2

1 Corinthians 3:1,2

Psalm 138:6

1 Corinthians 14:20

Proverbs 3:34

SPECIAL EXPERIENCES

1. Bring in baby pictures of all of the group members. Try to guess who is who.

2. Try and find positive affirming stories from a parent of each member. Tell the stories at the beginning of the study.

DISCUSSION STARTERS

1. Why is humility seemingly a tougher attitude to maintain than pride?

2. Charles Spurgeon once said that Psalm 131 "is one of the shortest psalms to read but one of the longest to learn." What do you think he meant by that?

3. What kind of problems come as a result of pride?

4. How do you feel about prideful people?

5. What positive things did you receive from your parents?

11. Obedience
Psalm 132

THE BIG IDEA

Believers living in obedience experience God's promises.

USING THE WORKBOOK

1. Educate the group in a proper historical understanding of the difference between Noah's Ark and the Ark of the Covenant. Exodus 25:10-22 helps to explain the Ark of the Covenant. If necessary, refer to a Bible encyclopedia, dictionary, or commentary for further background.

2. David made obedience to his task the top priority over the bare necessities of living. Help your group to see the extreme commitment on David's part.

3. Psalm 132:6-10 describes an in-depth search for the Ark of the Covenant. The Hebrews aggressively sought the place for God to dwell. Many modern-day Christians seem so passive when it comes to obedience. Develop some practical advice for your group's growth in obedience. Help them to find tasks to which they can be obedient.

4. David's obedience did not go unrewarded. The same promise exists today. We know of the promise in the life of Jesus Christ. It is a promise that carries with it more promises today.

RELATED SCRIPTURE

Micah 6:6-8   1 Samuel 15:10-23   Mark 12:28-34
Hosea 6:6

SPECIAL EXPERIENCES

1. Read 1 Samuel 15 and discuss God's response to Saul's disobedience.

2. Create a "Raiders of the Lost Ark" rally. Build an ark as a replica of the Ark of the Covenant. Place the ark in a certain location and give out clues for directions. Use Bible characters and Scripture for questions or clues. For example, "Drive on to as many streets as the number of times Peter denied Jesus before His death." Finish the rally with a study on the Ark or use this chapter.

DISCUSSION STARTERS

1. John Calvin wrote, "True knowledge of God is born out of obedience" (from *A Long Obedience in the Same Direction* by Eugene H. Peterson, p. 156). What do you think about this statement?

2. Why was the Ark so important to the Israelites?

3. What keeps you from being more obedient?

4. What comes to mind when you think of the word "obedient"?

5. Why might sacrifice be easier than obedience? (1 Samuel 15)

12. Unity
Psalm 133,134

THE BIG IDEA

Unity makes the Christian community stand out as an attractive refreshment for our dry world.

USING THE WORKBOOK

1. Unity is more than getting along. Unity is loving, caring, *and* getting along. One does not have to look far to find the disunity of our world. Read the reference verses found in Genesis, Matthew, Galatians, and Ephesians to emphasize the unity of God's children.

2. Psalm 133 provides two pictures of unity. One of them is unfamiliar to most Gentile, 20th century Christians. The chapter refers to Exodus to help explain the psalmist's words. The second analogy is easier to understand. Not only is community pleasant but it is essential for Christian growth. Church or fellowship is not optional.

3. The practice of unity begins with a believer's new attitude of refreshing others. List practical ways each member can live for unity.

4. Praise is a natural and necessary response to the unity God provides in our world. Psalm 134 invites the reader to celebrate unity and the many blessings received. The ten reasons to celebrate will hopefully be just the beginning of an overflowing attitude of praise to God for what He has done. Have each member share his answers to help others rejoice with him.

5. The chapter closes with John 17:20-23. Jesus prayed for the unity of believers. Help your group to see unity as a fulfillment of Jesus Christ's desires.

RELATED SCRIPTURE

Acts 2:1   Hebrews 10:25   Acts 5:12
Philippians 2:1-11   Philippians 4:4,5   John 17:6-16

SPECIAL EXPERIENCES

1. **Affirmation Experience**

   Few things build unity quicker than hearing from others how much
   they love and care for a person. Take a portion of time and have every
   person affirm the others for their positive qualities. Consider starting
   with one person holding the end of a ball of yarn. Have this person
   toss the ball to another person and affirm the recipient while still holding the end of the yarn. The second person holds on to their end and
   tosses the yarn to someone else including verbal affirmation. Make
   sure every person is affirmed. After a while the group should be inter-
   connected by the many weaves of the yarn. Use this as a picture of
   God's unified people.

2. End the group time with singing hymns, praises, praying, and Scripture
   reading. Begin and end the time with Psalm 134.

DISCUSSION STARTERS

1. What ingredients create unity?

2. What refreshes your life?

3. The best way to celebrate life is _____.

4. "Am I my brother's keeper?" How would Psalm 133 answer this
   question? Why?

5. Why is our world so disunified?